Material
Girls

Material Girls

Fabric Makeovers for Your Home

April Eden, Cat Wei, & Kelly Keener

A Division of Sterling Publishing Co., Inc.
New York / London

Series Editor: Candice Janco
Assistant Editor: Matt Paden
Contributing Writer: Susan Brill
Series Designer: Thom Gaines
Art Director: Thom Gaines
Cover Designer: DIY Network
Copy Editor: Jessica Boing

10 9 8 7 6 5 4 3 2 1

First Edition

Published by Lark Books, A Division of
Sterling Publishing Co., Inc.
387 Park Avenue South, New York, N.Y. 10016

Text © 2007, Lark Books
Design © 2007, Lark Books
Photography © 2007, DIY Network

Distributed in Canada by Sterling Publishing,
c/o Canadian Manda Group, 165 Dufferin Street
Toronto, Ontario, Canada M6K 3H6

Distributed in the United Kingdom by GMC Distribution Services,
Castle Place, 166 High Street, Lewes, East Sussex, England BN7 1XU

Distributed in Australia by Capricorn Link (Australia) Pty Ltd.,
P.O. Box 704, Windsor, NSW 2756 Australia

If you have questions or comments about this book, please contact:
Lark Books
67 Broadway
Asheville, NC 28801
(828) 253-0467

Manufactured in China

ISBN 13: 978-1-60059-183-9
ISBN 10: 1-60059-183-3

For information about custom editions,
special sales, premium and corporate purchases,
please contact Sterling Special Sales Department
at 800-805-5489 or specialsales@sterlingpub.com.

Contents

Material Girls

Welcome to *Material Girls*!

We are here to offer you the inspiration and expertise to transform your living space without buying new furniture or tearing down walls. With just a few yards of fabric, you can completely makeover a room, or your whole house!

While many people try to come up with a theme for a room and then find the fabric to match, we often find our inspiration in the fabric and let a great texture, color, or print develop into a theme for a whole room. Fabric is such a big part of interior design, yet many people don't realize the difference it makes.

Our DIY Network show, *Material Girls*, focuses on one room in a house. The only alteration we make is to paint the room to coordinate with the color scheme of the new design. We take the elements that are already in the room and breathe new life back into them with a little fabric. From giving an old wingback chair a faux slipcover to upholstering a coffee table that was headed for the trash, we give you ideas to remake what you have instead of buying something new.

The projects in this book will allow you to do that too—whether it's lending color and texture to a blank wall with a cornice board or a room screen; or sewing a comforter, bed skirt and canopy to transform a bedroom; or creating a welcoming home office that's both professional and warm. We're your source for projects that offer big results with just a few yards of fabric.

This book is divided into four chapters, each one full of step-by-step projects sure to inspire you. The first chapter, Bedrooms, features ideas to turn your sleeping space into an relaxing space. The second chapter, Living Rooms, focuses on ways to make the most of the rooms where you entertain, relax, or spend family time. The third chapter, Kids' Rooms, covers ideas from newborn to teen for creative young environments. The fourth chapter, Work Rooms, includes projects to warm up the productive spaces in your house, from home office to study to kitchen.

You probably already have many of the materials you need to begin transforming your space. Some projects require a sewing machine, but there are also plenty of others that can be completed with just a staple gun or fabric glue.

We hope this book inspires you to be creative with your living spaces, and gives you ideas to take what you already have and make it beautiful!

Cat Wei, Kelly Keener, & April Eden,
hosts of DIY *Material Girls*

1

Bedrooms

Whether you are looking for a design that's romantic, tranquil, or sophisticated, this chapter has bedroom ideas for you. It's full of creative projects to transform an ordinary bedroom into an inviting, restful sanctuary. Go all out with a floating canopy and coordinating duvet cover, bed skirt, and pillows. Or keep it simple with side table runners, covered lamp shades, and covered switch plates. You're sure to find a project here to inspire a new look for a tired bedroom in need of a change.

FEMININE SOPHISTICATE

With her two sons all grown up, this mom was ready to give her home a more feminine touch where she could relax and enjoy hobbies and reading.

BEFORE: All this bedroom had going for it was a great four-poster bed.

PROJECT SUMMARY

The Material Girls turned this bedroom into a feminine, but sophisticated, soothing space with lots of toile and a selection of soft pink, cream, and tan fabrics. They made a wall canopy, sewed an elegant London shade for a window, made a round tablecloth for a side table, and covered a switch plate for a complete, coordinated look.

AFTER: A wall canopy with a fabric valance and cloth panels gives a softness to the room and accents the bed overhead.

Fabric and Color Swatches

AFTER: Decorator pillows and a short table runner for an antique cabinet blend French country and elegant silk.

LONDON SHADE

This London shade is a feminine window cover with two vertical ties to hold folds of fabric in a gentle swoop, fanned at the sides. You'll sew the lined curtain with a rod pocket, make the ties, and then adjust the length and billow of the fabric to your taste before you install it.

You Will Need

Measuring tape	Iron
Fabric	Sewing machine and thread
Lining	Curtain rod
Scissors	
Straight pins	

1 Measure the size of the window. Add 15 extra inches for folds at the bottom of the shade, and 6 extra inches at the top for the rod pocket, as well as enough on each side for a hem. Cut the fabric and lining to size.

1 Measure the size of the window. Add 15 extra inches for folds at the bottom of the shade, and 6 extra inches at the top for the rod pocket, as well as enough on each side for a hem. Cut the fabric and lining to size.

2 Place the lining and fabric with wrong sides together. Fold one side in about 3 inches (photo A), and tuck under the raw edge (photo B). Press and pin the side hem (photo C). Repeat on the other side.

3 Double fold the bottom hem up about 4 inches (photo D). Press and pin in place. Sew the side and bottom hems.

TIPS | DIY Network Crafts

HEMMING SHADES

Use a double, 4-inch hem (4 inches turned in twice) at the bottom of a curtain or shade, and a double 1½-inch hem on the sides for the fabric to hang nicely with enough weight.

4 Fold the top in about 3 inches (photo E). Fold in again and press. The rod pocket will be made with this fold later.

5 For the ties, cut four strips of fabric 6 inches longer than the length of the shade in the width desired. Fold the raw edges in about ½ inch and press (photo F).

6 Fold the fabric in half lengthwise and press. Then fold one end in (photo G), stitch across the end and down the length of each strip.

7 Each tie has two parts--one for the front of the shade and one for the back. Lay two ties together with raw edges even. Tuck the raw edges under the rod pocket, positioned 5 to 8 inches in from the side (photo H). Position the other pair of ties on the same distance from the other side of the shade. (The further apart the ties, the deeper the shade will swoop in the middle.)

8 Fold one tie of each set over the hem and to the front of the shade (photo I). Pin the top, and sew a straight stitch all the way across.

9 Fold the bottom of the fabric like a fan (photo J) and make decorative bows or knots with the ties to hold the material in place.

WALL CANOPY

Build a cornice board and wrap it with batting and fabric to create a soft, overhead accent for a bed. Staples hold the fabric in place, and L-brackets secure the valance to the wall. If desired, sew fabric panels to add another layer to the cornice board as well.

You Will Need

Measuring tape	Staple gun and staples
Plywood, pre-cut	Fabric (2 coordinating prints)
Drill	Scissors
Wood screws	4 L-brackets (2 sizes)
Batting	Coordinating cording

1 Determine the size of the valance based on the width of the bed. In this case, the side pieces are 10 inches and the top is 60 inches wide. Pre-cut the wood to size.

2 Pre-drill the holes for the screws, and attach the boards with wood screws (photo A) to make the cornice board.

3 Tightly stretch batting over the front and sides of the board, and staple it in place (photo B). Batting helps soften the edges of the wood and give a more feminine look. Fold in the corners of the batting and secure it with staples.

4 Wrap fabric over the cornice board. Secure one edge of the fabric to the board with staples. Wrap the fabric snugly without stretching it too much. Tuck any excess fabric in at the corners of the board and staple it in place (photo C). Fold the raw edge of the remaining side under to create a hem, and staple it in place (photo D).

5 Secure two L-brackets in the corners with screws to give the cornice board support. Then mount a larger L-bracket on each side to attach the canopy to the wall.

6 For a more dramatic look, staple panels of a second fabric on top. Sew panels with cording in the seams and join them together along the top with another long piece of cording. To attach the panels, carefully line them up with the corners of the cornice board, and staple the top edge of the panels to the inside top edge of the cornice (photo E). The panels should hang slightly longer than the cornice board (photo F).

7 Attach the valance to the wall with the L-brackets and screws on each side. Add matching curtains behind for added softness and texture.

TIPS | DIY Network Crafts

INTERESTING CONTRAST

Using contrasting fabric panels over the fabric valance allows the print beneath to peek through, adding depth and visual interest to the canopy.

TABLE ROUNDS

This simple round tablecloth will transform any unsightly bedside table. Just measure the table, mark and cut the fabric, and sew a simple hem. It's a quick and easy solution.

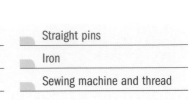

You Will Need

Cloth measuring tape	Straight pins
Fabric	Iron
Fabric chalk	Sewing machine and thread
Scissors	

1 Measure the width of the tabletop and the height of the table from the floor. Double the height and add the width, plus several inches for the hem. Divide the total measurement in half. For this project, the result was 27 inches.

2 Fold the fabric in half lengthwise, and then fold it in half again, crosswise (photo A). The double-folded corner will be the center of the tablecloth.

3 Holding a cloth tape measure at the center corner and fabric chalk at the designated mark on the measuring tape, draw an arch from one end of the fabric to the other (photo B). Cut through all four layers of the fabric along the mark.

4 Fold in a hem about ¼ inch around the edge of the circle (photo C). Then fold the hem again to hide the raw edges. Pin and press in place. Sew the hem with a straight stitch.

TIPS | DIY Network Crafts

ADDING WIDTH

If your fabric isn't wide enough for the measurement in step 1, sew two pieces together. To avoid having a seam down the center, cut one of the pieces of fabric in half and sew a half on each side of the center piece, matching the fabric pattern as closely as possible.

COVERED SWITCH PLATE

Add a coordinating detail of color and texture to a room by covering the light switch plate with fabric. A little fabric, glue, and a utility knife are all you need.

You Will Need

Switch plate	Fabric glue
Fabric	Utility knife
Scissors	Nail
Spray adhesive	

1 Cut the fabric to the size of the switch plate, plus one inch on all sides.

2 Spray the front of the switch plate with adhesive, and center it onto the wrong side of the fabric (photo A).

3 Fold the edges of the fabric around the sides of the plate, securing it to the back with fabric glue.

4 Make an X with a craft knife from the back of the plate in the hole for the switch (photo B).

5 Glue the fabric corners in place on the back of the plate.

6 Attach the plate to the wall with screws.

TIPS | DIY Network Crafts

PROTECT THE FABRIC

Use a nail to poke through the fabric for the screw holes so the ridges of the screw don't run or tear the fabric.

FINISHING TOUCHES

Blend French country and elegant fine silks with a comforter for the bed, pillow shams (see Flanged Pillow Sham, page 32) and decorative pillows (see Decorative Pillows, page 50), as well as a bed skirt (see Box-Pleated Bed Skirt, page 24). Create linen or silk table runners (see Table Runner, page 28) to add elegance to antique furniture, and add votive candles to make the room glow.

ISLAND OASIS

As the busy parents of five children, Bob and Dianna have very little time to themselves. They needed a romantic bedroom getaway!

BEFORE: Bare walls and plain windows left this bedroom lacking interest or charm.

AFTER: Relaxing and unique, the room is now like a tropical getaway.

Fabric and Color Swatches

PROJECT SUMMARY

The Material Girls drew upon this couple's love of the Caribbean to create a tranquil island oasis filled with soothing colors and luxurious tropical fabrics. They made a box-pleated skirt for the bed with a floating canopy above, covered a lampshade, and crafted an easy, no-sew table runner.

AFTER: A floating canopy over the bed and soothing tropical prints and colors turn this room into a restful oasis.

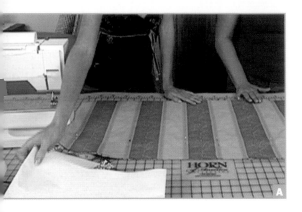

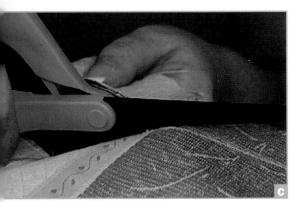

FLOATING BED CANOPY

Make your own scallop pattern and sew a self-lining canopy in this project. You'll hang the canopy with curtain rods and tassels from hooks in the ceiling when you're done.

You Will Need

Fabric	Plate or saucer	2 curtain rods
Scissors	Sewing machine	4 ceiling hooks
Scrap paper	Needle and thread	4 long tassels
Fabric chalk	Iron	
Measuring tape	Straight pins	

1 Measure the bed and the wall to decide the size for the canopy in proportion to it. Cut two pieces of fabric the desired length of the canopy. Cut two smaller pieces for the scalloped valance on the front of the canopy (photo A).

2 Make a paper pattern for the scalloped valance: Cut a piece of paper the size of your material. Position a plate or saucer on the narrow end of the paper, at the edge (see Calculating Scallops, page 121, to determine the size of plate to trace). Trace around the plate. Move the plate next to and just touching the circle traced. Trace the next circle. Continue to the edge of the paper. Use scissors to clip along the bottom edges of the circles to create a scalloped edge.

3 Lay the valance fabric with right sides together. Pin the pattern to the fabric, and trace around it with fabric chalk (photo B).

4 Sew the top and sides of the valance, leaving a gap in the seam large enough to turn the valance right side out.

5 Carefully sew around the scalloped edge. Cut around the scallop as close to the stitching as possible (photo C). Turn the fabric right side out and press.

6 Lay one piece of the canopy material face up and lay the valance on top of it, raw edges together. Lay the other piece of canopy material face down on top of the valance. Line it up evenly. Pin in place, and stitch across the top.

7 Stitch the sides of the canopy, making sure not to catch the valance material in the seam (photo D). Leave a 2-inch opening at the top for the rod pockets, and another opening 2 feet down for the other rod pocket (or adjust the position according to how you will hang your canopy).

8 With a ruler and chalk, draw a straight line across the canopy at the openings for the top rod pocket (photo E). Repeat for the bottom rod pocket. Sew a straight stitch along each chalk line.

9 To attach the canopy to the ceiling, anchor four hooks into the ceiling: two hooks above the head-board and the other hooks 2 feet out from the headboard.

10 Insert the curtain rods into the pockets of the canopy. Use decorative tassels to tie the rod finials to the hooks (photo F).

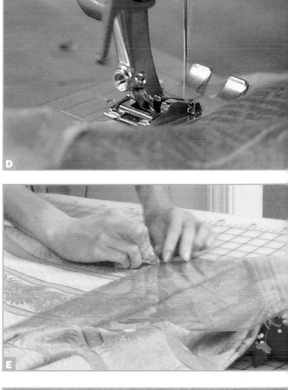

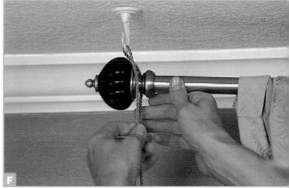

TIPS | DIY Network Crafts

SCALLOPING FABRIC
Instead of creating a pattern for the scalloped edge of the valance, trace half of the plate directly onto the fabric with fabric chalk if desired.

BOX-PLEATED BED SKIRT

Make a decorative bed skirt that is simply pinned in place onto the box spring.

You Will Need

Measuring tape	Sewing machine and thread
Decorative fabric for skirt	Iron
Plain fabric for band	Straight pins
Scissors	Safety pins

1 Measure the length of the sides and footboard of the bed. Multiply each measurement by 4 to allow plenty of fabric for the pleats. Cut three pieces of fabric according to those lengths--one for the footboard and one for each side (photo A).

2 Cut plain fabric for the band--cutting four pieces the length of the bed plus 4 inches, and cutting two pieces the length of the footboard plus 4 inches. Set the band pieces aside.

3 With the footboard skirt fabric, fold up the bottom hem about 3 inches (photo B). Fold the raw edge inside the hem, and press (photo C).

4 Pin along the folded line and sew a straight stitch all the way across (photo D). Then iron the hem for a smooth look.

5 Choose the width of the pleats, taking into account the pattern of the fabric. This project used 12-inch-wide pleats with the pineapple image on the fabric as the center of each pleat.

6 Create the first pleat, measuring the width and making sure the pattern is centered. Fold the sides of the pleat under several inches (photo E). Pin in place securely so the pleat will not shift as you work.

7 Create the second pleat, measuring the width and tucking under the sides so that the fold of the second pleat touches the first. Pin all of the pleats in place; then press them with an iron for a nice, straight fold (photo F). Sew a straight stitch across the top of the material.

8 Fold one fabric band for the footboard in half lengthwise. Press with an iron. Open it and place it on the wrong side of the top edge of the bed skirt, matching raw edges (photo G). Stitch in place.

9 Fold the band on the crease, turn under the raw edge (photo H), and pin the band to the right side of the skirt. Topstitch the band to the skirt along the bottom edge of the band. Tuck in the extra fabric on each end and stitch it closed.

10 Repeat steps 3 through 10 for the side pieces of the bed skirt. Secure the skirt to the box spring with safety pins.

COVERED LAMPSHADE

Add a coordinating element to the room, or a splash of color, with a fabric-covered lampshade. It requires only a little fabric, scissors, and fabric glue—no sewing! Be sure to use a heat-safe fabric for this project.

You Will Need

Fabric	Scissors
Lampshade	Fabric glue
Fabric chalk or marker	

1 Lay the fabric on your workspace and roll the lampshade on its side across the fabric to ensure that you have enough fabric (photo A). Use the lampshade's seam as the guide that your roll is complete.

2 Lay the lampshade on the wrong side of the fabric. Starting at one corner of the fabric, roll the shade across the fabric, marking the fabric at the top of the shade as you go (photo B). Repeat to mark the fabric at the bottom of the shade. Use a ruler to join the top mark to the bottom mark, and cut out the fabric.

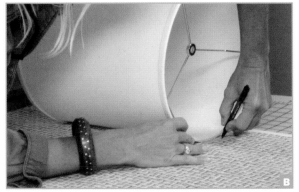

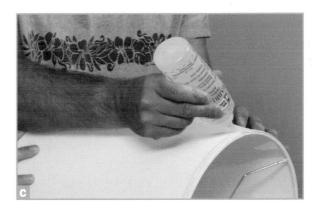

3 Position the lampshade, seam side up, in the center of the wrong side of the fabric. Run a bead line of fabric glue along the seam of the lampshade (photo C), and wrap one side of the fabric around the shade to the seam. Press the edge of the fabric in place on the glue.

4 Run another beaded line of glue where the fabric will overlap (photo D). Fold the edge of the fabric under for a cleaner look, and press the fabric in place.

5 Run a line of glue around the top inside rim of the shade, and fold the fabric in, pressing into place. Repeat this process on the bottom of the shade. Trim any excess fabric.

TIPS | DIY Network Crafts

LAMPSHADE WIRES

To help the fabric fold nicely over the top of the shade, make two cuts in the fabric at each metal support on the shade. Press the fabric into the bead of glue on either side of the metal, and trim off the fabric remnant.

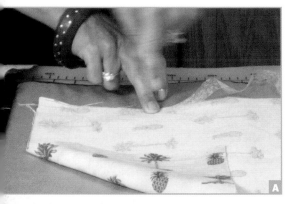

TABLE RUNNER

This is another easy, no-sew project to add coordinating color and softness to the room with fabric. Fusible tape and an iron make this project quick and easy.

You Will Need

Measuring tape	Iron
Fabric	Ironing board
Scissors	Tassels (optional)
Fusible tape	

1 Measure the fabric to the desired size, adding about 1 extra inch on all sides. The runner shown is 12 x 40 inches. Cut the fabric to size.

2 Place the fabric face down on an ironing board. Line the fusible tape along the edge (photo A) and fold the fabric over the tape to create a hem. Use another piece of fabric as a pressing cloth to keep any residual adhesive from sticking to the iron (photo B).

3 Hold the iron on the edge of the fabric for about 5 to 10 seconds; this will cause the tape to bond. Repeat on all sides.

TIPS | DIY Network
Crafts

A SEAMLESS FINISH

Even if you like to sew, you may want to complete this project with fusible tape, especially if you have a patterned fabric and don't want stitching to show. The tape will create seamless hems for a finished look.

4 On the raw-edge ends of the fabric, measure and mark the center point. Then, measure 6 inches down each side and mark at the edges (photo C). Fold the fabric from side dots to center dot, forming a point. Keep a seam allowance the width of the fusible tape, and cut off the excess at the corner (photo D).

5 Lay fusible tape in place under the hem on the pointed end and fuse with an iron. Repeat for both ends.

6 For an added decorative touch, glue tassels onto each end of the table runner (photo E).

FINISHING TOUCHES

Add decorative pillows (see Tufted Round Pillow and Designer Pillows, pages 36 and 37) and a cream comforter to add a focal point in the bedroom. Add a cushion (see Hearth Box Cushion, page 54) to a trunk. And dress the windows with a single panel curtain and valance (see Unlined Rod-Pocket Curtains, page 44 and Valance, page 58).

MASTER BEDROOM MAKEOVER

Jerri and George's floor-to-ceiling windows afforded them a great view of the outdoors in their master bedroom, and they wanted to bring that outdoor feeling inside. First, they needed some help knowing where to start this bedroom makeover.

BEFORE: This bedroom had a great view but lacked any other ambiance or interest.

AFTER: Coordinating bed coverings, a fabric panel floor screen, and fabric wall art transform this space into a tranquil retreat.

PROJECT SUMMARY

The Material Girls used fabrics in the colors of nature and turned this plain bedroom into a tranquil retreat. They used an abstract rose pattern in ivory, sage green, and mocha brown for the color scheme, with richly textured coordinating fabrics for the bed and a new soothing green shade of paint on the walls for a spa feeling. They made a coordinating duvet cover and flanged pillow shams and built a floor screen from scratch to add color and texture to the room.

Fabric and Color Swatches

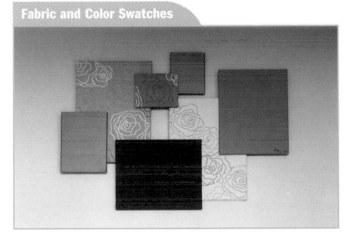

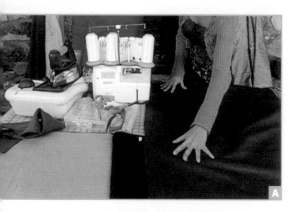

FLANGED PILLOW SHAM

Sew flanged pillow shams with contrasting fabrics and cording, such as the rich brown for the flange and the embroidered ivory fabric for the center used here.

You Will Need

Measuring tape	Straight pins
Pillow	Cording
Fabric, 2 colors	Cording foot or zipper foot
Scissors	Sewing machine and thread

1 Measure the size of the pillow, and add 1½ inches to the length and the width for the seam allowances. Cut a panel for the center of the pillow to these dimensions.

2 Cut the flange piece larger in each dimension than the center piece, according to the desired size for the finished sham (photo A).

3 To size the back of the sham, start with the measurements used for the front flange piece. Add 10 inches to the length to allow for the opening. Measure the fabric, and cut the piece for the back of the sham. Then, cut the length of the back piece of the sham in half, directly down the middle (photo B).

4 Pin the cording to the right side of the front panel of the sham (photo C). Notch the corners as you go (photo D). Using a cording foot or zipper foot, sew on the cording.

SERGING RAW EDGES

If your sewing machine has a serger, serge the edges of the fabric pieces before sewing them together in this project. Serging keeps the edges of fabric from fraying. The serger cuts the raw edges of the fabric and finishes the edge with stitching all in one step. This is important for pieces that get a lot of use, such as pillows.

5 To make the back piece of the sham, fold the edge of one back piece over about 1 inch on the center cut, tucking the raw edge under (photo E). Press the fold with an iron. Pin to hold it in place, and then stitch (photo F). Fold the other back piece of the sham in about 3 inches on the center cut, and follow the same procedure.

6 Matching up the edges, lay the back pieces onto the front piece with right sides together. (The back two pieces should overlap with the wider, 3-inch, hemmed piece laying under the 1-inch, hemmed piece). Pin around all four edges in place and sew.

7 Remove all of the pins, and turn the pillow sham right side out. Press the sham with an iron so the corners and the edges lay flat (photo G).

8 Lay the sham with the front piece facing up. Center the contrasting fabric over the flange piece, with the wrong side of the contrasting fabric down, facing the right side of the flange (photo H). Use a tape measure to center the piece exactly. Carefully pin it in place, tucking under the raw edge so the cording forms the edge of the center piece. Position the pins to allow the sewing machine to sew easily over them (photo I).

9 Using a zipper foot, and moving the needle of the machine slightly to the right, follow the cording and stitch as closely as possible to it.

10 Turn the sham over and insert a pillow into the pocket on the back.

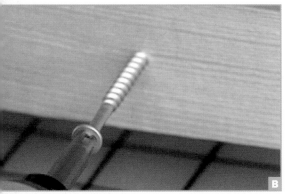

CORNER SCREEN

A fabric screen adds texture and softens the look of a room, especially one with wood floors or wood furniture. Make two fabric-covered panels for this screen, and then join them with cabinet hinges.

You Will Need

5 2 x 2s cut to desired size (per panel)	Fabric
	Scissors
Drill	Staple gun
2½" wood screws	Hinges

1 Lay the 2 x 2s in place for the frame, including a center board for a brace positioned halfway down the height of the screen.

2 Pre-drill holes at least ¾ inch away from the edge of the wood on each corner to prevent the wood from splitting. Make sure to hold the boards flush so that they will not snag the fabric or create a bump (photo A). Pre-drill holes for the center brace as well.

3 Join the frame with 2½-inch wood screws through the pre-drilled holes, making sure each joint is flush (photo B).

4 Cut the fabric allowing several inches on each side of the frame to turn the raw edge under twice and wrap to the back of the frame. If you use a patterned fabric, as in this project, make sure to match the pattern when you cut the pieces (see Matching the Fabric Pattern, page 44).

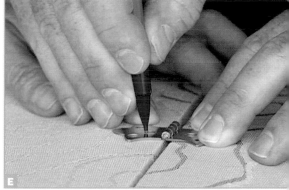

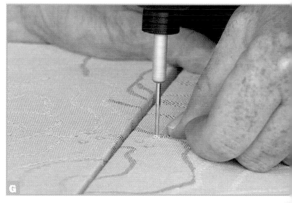

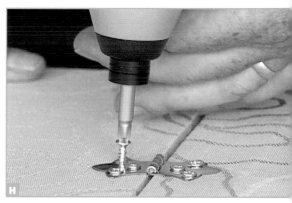

5 Stretch the fabric tightly over the frame, and staple the folded edge in place on the back side (photo C). Work around the frame, keeping the fabric pulled taut and working out any wrinkles along the way. Leave the corners for last.

6 At the corners, fold the fabric in tightly, as though wrapping a package. Staple the first layer of fabric in place, and then pull the remaining fabric over and staple it in place as well (photo D). Be sure to make a straight line at the corner for a finished look. Trim any excess material.

7 Repeat steps 1 through 6 for the desired number of panels for the screen. Lay the panels side-by-side to join them. Make sure they are positioned to match the fabric, if necessary.

8 Measure 6 inches from the top of the frame and lay one hinge in place. Mark the holes for the screws (photo E). Measure 6 inches further for the next hinge; mark the holes. Position two hinges for the bottom of the screen in the same manner.

9 Use a hammer and a nail to punch holes in the fabric before predrilling the frame for screws in step 10 (photo F). This helps keep the fabric from fraying or getting caught in the drill bit.

10 Predrill the holes for the screws (photo G), and attach the hinges with screws (photo H).

FABRIC WALL ART

Cover canvases with fabric and secure them together with screws to make a collage of fabrics to tie together and accent any room.

You Will Need

- Coordinating fabrics
- Canvas-covered frames (various sizes)
- Scissors
- Staple gun and staples
- Drill
- Screws

1 Lay the canvas frame on the wrong side of the fabric, squaring the frame with the grain of the fabric. Cut around the frame with enough margin to wrap the fabric to the back edge of the canvas.

2 Staple the fabric to the back, beginning in the middle of one side and working your way toward a corner. Alternate sides as you go, and leave the corners for last.

3 Miter the corners with a neat fold, and staple down. Trim the excess fabric close to the line of staples.

4 Repeat steps 1 through 3 on canvases of various sizes, using complementary fabrics. Arrange the covered canvases in formation for hanging. Secure them together by drilling small screws in through the back of the frames.

TUFTED ROUND PILLOW

This round pillow is an easy accent to make for any room. Use polyester fiberfill to stuff it, then tuft with buttons in the center.

You Will Need

- Fabric
- Scissors
- Cording
- Straight pins
- Sewing machine and thread
- Cording foot or zipper foot
- Polyester fiberfill
- Needle and thread
- Upholstery needle
- 2 large buttons

1 Cut two pieces of fabric the desired size for the pillow, adding 1 inch for the seam allowances.

2 Lay the front and back pieces with right sides together, matching any pattern or direction of the fabric. Tuck the cording between the layers, and pin the raw edges of the pillow and cording together.

3 Sew all three pieces together using a zipper foot, removing pins as you go. Leave a gap of several inches for turning.

4 Turn the pillow right side out and stuff firmly with polyester fiberfill. Then, hand stitch the opening closed with cording in place.

5 Push a threaded upholstery needle through the center of the pillow from back to front. Thread the needle through a button on the front side. Push the needle back through the same hole to the back. Thread the needle through a button on the back. Pull the two thread ends tightly, creating a dimple in the pillow, and knot the threads together.

PIECED DESIGNER PILLOW

Add decorative pillows that pull together all of the elements of your decor by piecing fabrics from around the room. Use a pillow form to make this pillow.

You Will Need

Various fabrics	Decorative cording
Pillow foam	Sewing machine and thread
Scissors	Cording foot or zipper foot
Gimp trim	Needle and thread
Straight pins	

1 Cut two pieces of fabric to the size of the pillow form for the pillow front and back, adding 1 inch to each dimension for the seam allowances.

2 Cut smaller squares or strips of the other fabrics and arrange them in place on the front fabric, overlapping. Lay strips of gimp trim over each seam, covering the raw edges, and pin through all layers.

3 Stitch two seams on each strip of gimp, down each of the long edges, to secure the layers together.

4 Lay the back and front pillow pieces with right sides together. Tuck cording between the front and back on each side, keeping raw edges even. Pin three sides, leaving the length of cording for the fourth side hanging.

5 Stitch the three pinned sides using a cording or zipper foot to stitch close to the cording. Turn the pillow right side out, and insert the pillow form. Pin the fourth side closed with the cording in place. Hand stitch closed.

TIPS DIY Network Crafts

SEWING LAYERS

When sewing several layers of fabric together, be sure to use a long stitch to prevent puckering.

DUVET COVER

The front of this duvet cover is decorative fabric and the back is cotton lining. Sew them together with trim, and secure with snap tape.

You Will Need

Measuring tape	Coordinating thread
Fabric	Straight pins
Scissors	Iron
Serger (optional)	Snap tape
Sewing machine	Zipper foot

1 Depending on the size of the bed, cut either two or three pieces of fabric from the bolt using the full width of the fabric. If your bed requires only two pieces of fabric, center one panel and cut the other panel in half, placing one half on each side of the center panel. This prevents the need for a seam down the center of the cover.

2 Serge the pieces for the cover if you have a sewing machine with a serger (photo A). Then, sew the panels together, making sure the pattern is right side up on all pieces and matching the pattern at the seams.

3 Fold a double 2½-inch hem on the bottom of the duvet panel, and press it with an iron. Pin the pressed edge, and sew in place (photo B).

TIPS | DIY Network Crafts

SERGER ALTERNATIVE

If your sewing machine does not have a serger, cut the raw edges of the fabric with pinking sheers to defer raveling.

TIPS | DIY Network Crafts

MASK A MISMATCH WITH TRIM

If you are unable to match the fabric pattern at the seam, sew a decorative trim such as gimp into the seam. This adds elegance and draws the eye away from a slight mismatch in the panels. Use a zipper foot on your sewing machine to attach the gimp trim.

4 Repeat steps 1 through 4 for the back of the duvet with the cotton lining fabric.

5 Match up the seams of the front and back of the cover, wrong sides together. Separate the length of snap tape, and position one layer on the top hem of the front and back center panels of the cover. Pin in place, double checking to make sure the front and back seams are still aligned. Stitch along the edge of the snap tape using a zipper foot (photo C). Make sure that the seams of the front and back still line up and sew the second tape into place.

6 Lay the front and back of the duvet cover with right sides together. Line up the seams and snap tape. Pin all of the edges together. Sew the front and back together, except for the section with the snaps.

7 Turn the cover inside out, insert the comforter, and snap the top closed.

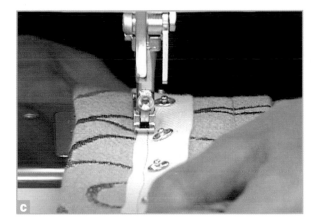

TIPS | DIY Network Crafts

KEEPING EVERYTHING IN PLACE

Add ties at each corner of the duvet cover and on the comforter to keep the comforter from shifting inside. Using ribbons, twill tape, or strips of fabric for ties, stitch them into the seam allowances. Then, use a knot or bow to tie them together.

FINISHING TOUCHES

Tuck three, square-sham pillows behind the sewn Flanged Shams to add dimension and give a fuller, luxurious look. Then sew sheer curtains (see Unlined Rod-Pocket Curtains, page 44) that will add softness to the windows without obstructing the light.

2

Living Rooms

If you love to spend time as a family in your home, or enjoy entertaining others, this chapter has ideas to make the most of the living room or family room you have. No matter what you start with, you can make small spaces seem bigger, warm up cool modern design, or heat up ordinary into hip. These projects are sure to inspire.

WARMING UP MODERN

Ron and Sara fell in love with their contemporary house for its clean lines and minimalist exterior. But the interior is a different story. The hard surfaces, industrial materials, and lack of color left them wanting more. They decided to inject some warmth and color into their living space.

BEFORE: This austere modern house had a great view and beautiful lines that just needed warming up.

AFTER: Warm, floral-patterned curtains add drama and color, while padded ottomans and throw pillows soften the room for an inviting ambiance.

Fabric and Color Swatches

◢ PROJECT SUMMARY ◣

The Material Girls drew upon this couple's love of nature and the outdoors, infusing the space with rich autumn tones of brown, green, and orange. They used simple curtain panels to disguise storage areas, built a padded ottoman from scratch, and added throw pillows and a micro-suede table mat to help make this space warm, soft, and colorful.

MATCHING THE FABRIC PATTERN

If your fabric has a distinct pattern, be sure to cut the curtain panels so the patterns match from panel to panel. Here's how:

1 Look at the length of fabric and find where the pattern ends and begins again. Measure the length of one occurrence of the pattern from start to finish. This is the "repeat." The fabric used in this project had a 53-inch repeat.

2 Plan on enough fabric to use full repeats for each panel. For instance, in this project, 93¼ inches were needed for the curtain, so each panel was cut from two repeats, or 106 inches of fabric.

3 Starting at the same point in the pattern on each section of fabric, cut out each curtain panel. This allows the curtains to have a uniform appearance when hung.

UNLINED ROD-POCKET CURTAINS

Curtains are an easy disguise for a bank of closets in any room. These curtains are simple panels with a casing—rod pocket—sewn at the top to accommodate a curtain rod for hanging, two side hems, and a bottom hem. In this case, the bi-fold doors on the closets were removed, and the curtain rods were mounted inside the door frame.

You Will Need

Curtain rod	Fabric chalk or pencil
Mounting hardware	Scissors
Measuring tape	Sewing machine and thread
Electric screwdriver	Iron and ironing board
Fabric	Straight pins

1 Using the mounting kit that comes with the curtain rod, install the hardware for the curtain rod on the wall.

2 To determine the finished length of the curtain panels, measure from the top of the rod to the floor. Then, measure the width of the curtain rod (photo A). To allow material for the rod pocket, double the width of the rod and add 1 inch for the seam allowance and ¼ inch for "take up"—the amount of fabric the curtain takes to go over the rod. Then add 8 inches for the curtain hem.

A

CALCULATE!

Taking accurate measurements can be the hardest part of sewing. You may want to have a calculator on hand to be double sure of your calculations before you cut and sew.

3 Cut the fabric to size and lay it out on the table. Measure and mark 8 inches from the bottom of the panel in several places (photo B).

4 Fold up the bottom hem 4 inches, and fold over 4 inches again. Pin in place and press with an iron, making sure the fold aligns with the marks made. Sew the hem with a straight stitch.

5 For the side hems, measure and mark 3 inches in on the side of the panel in several places (photo C). Fold in 1½ inches and press. Turn over 1½ inches more, pin in place, and sew with a straight stitch. This is called the "Double 1½."

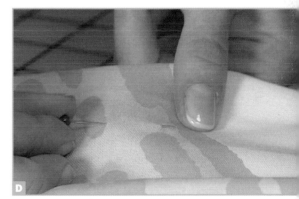

6 Mark the fold for the rod pocket as determined in step 2, and fold half of the length in. Press on the fold, and fold in again on the line marked for a double fold. This creates a stiff pocket so the curtain lays flat. Pin the rod pocket in place (photo D), press, and sew with a straight stitch through all of the layers.

7 Insert the curtain rod into the rod pocket and hang.

You Will Need

- 4 17" x 13½" pine or fir plywood
- 2 17" x 2" x 2" boards
- 1½" deck screws
- 2 17" x17" pine or fir plywood
- Drill and screwdriver bits
- 18" x 18" x 2" upholstery-grade foam
- 18" x 18" x 1" upholstery-grade foam
- Electric carving knife
- Spray adhesive

◢ BUILDING A CUBE OTTOMAN ◣

Build a custom-sized plywood box for this ottoman, cover it with foam, and sew a micro-suede cover to finish it off. The finished ottoman measures 18 x 18 x 19½ inches, but adjust the measurements to any size you like. Use 1-inch pine or fir plywood for this project.

1 Begin with the four 17 x 13-inch boards for the sides. Lay them out on the work surface and lay the 2 x 2s on the same side of each board (photo A). These are the supports that make the box strong enough to hold a seated person.

2 To attach the supports, flip over the plywood, flush up the 2 x 2s underneath, and attach with 1½-inch deck screws (photo B).

TIPS | DIY Network Crafts

EXTRA-STRONG JOINTS
For extra strength in the joints of the ottoman, put a little wood glue along the edge of the 2 x 2 when you attach it to the side panel. Then, add L-brackets as well to support the sides and the top.

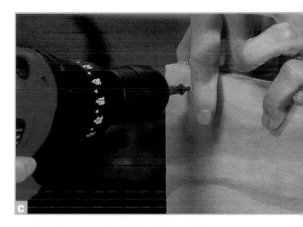

TIPS | DIY Network
Crafts

BUYING AND SIZING POLYFOAM

High density polyfoam—upholstery-grade foam—
is available at foam outlet or home stores. It
comes in rolls or large pieces, so you will need to
cut it to size. Use an electric carving knife to
make quick, clean cuts in the polyfoam.

3 Join the side pieces together by holding two sides in
place at the corner and installing 1½-inch screws
through the plywood and into the 2 x 2 supports (photo C).

4 Attach the top and bottom boards the same way,
using the 17 x 17-inch pieces of plywood (photo D).
Make sure to install the screws into the ends of the 2 x 2
supports underneath.

5 Spray one side piece of the foam with adhesive.
Spray the side of the ottoman cube with adhesive as
well for extra strength. Position the foam to hang 1 inch
off each side and 2 inches off the top of the side panel.
Press the foam to the side panel firmly (photo E).

6 Spray one side of the 2-inch foam with adhesive;
spray the plywood top with adhesive as well. Press
the top foam piece into place.

TIPS | DIY Network
Crafts

SAFETY ALERT

Use spray adhesive in a well-ventilated area to
avoid breathing the fumes. Follow any safety
precautions on the label.

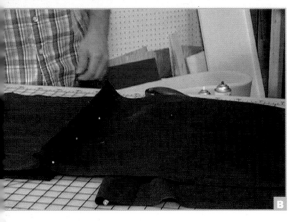

You Will Need

Measuring tape	Upholstery regulator
Micro-suede fabric	Staple gun and staples
Fabric chalk or pencil	Drill and screwdriver bits
Rotary cutter or scissors	4 4" furniture legs and bracket hardware
Sewing machine and thread	

MAKING THE OTTOMAN COVER

1 Measure the top and sides of the padded ottoman cube. Add a ½-inch seam allowance to each edge (1 inch to the length and width of the fabric pieces).

2 Measure and mark the micro-suede fabric to size. This project used four pieces $18\frac{5}{8}$ x $21\frac{1}{8}$ inches, and one piece $18\frac{5}{8}$ x $18\frac{5}{8}$ inches. Cut the micro-suede fabric as marked using a rotary cutter (photo A) or a scissors.

3 Mark the pieces with a fabric pencil, "T" for top and "S" for sides, on the wrong side of the fabric.

4 Pin the side pieces together with right sides facing (photo B). Sew all of the sides seams with a straight stitch.

5 Pin the top piece to the edges of the four side panels, right sides together. Sew the top in place starting about 6 inches from one corner. (It is harder to make all seams meet if you start sewing right at the corner.)

TIPS | DIY Network Crafts

WHICH SIDE IS UP?

Micro-suede has a rough texture on the front side and a smooth texture on the back. Make sure the nap on each side piece goes in the same direction when you position the pieces for sewing, and make sure to pin rough sides together.

6 As you come to a corner, stop ½ inch from the edge, leaving the needle in the fabric. Raise the presser foot, and turn the fabric 90 degrees, into position for the next seam (photo C). Lower the foot again, and continue sewing the next side. Work each seam and corner this way until you reach the starting point.

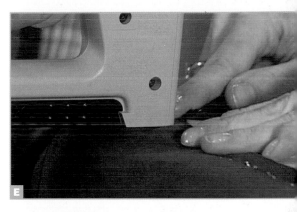

7 Turn the cover right side out, and lay the fabric on top of the foam. Work the sides of the fabric down over the ottoman a few inches at a time.

8 Use a regulator to pull the corners out evenly (photo D), being careful to keep the regulator pointed away from you.

9 Wrap the bottom edge of the fabric around the bottom of the ottoman and staple in place on the plywood. Fold the material at the corners as though wrapping a present, making it lay as flat as possible. Secure the corners with staples (photo E).

10 Attach foot brackets about 1½ inches in from the corners of the ottoman, securing through the fabric. Avoid hitting the staples (photo F). Screw pre-painted feet to the foot brackets.

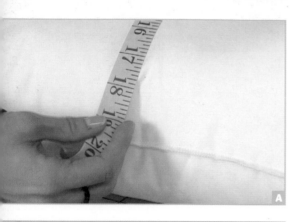

◗ DECORATIVE PILLOWS ◗

Make a variety of simple throw pillows from various fabrics such as faux fur and silk dupioni to add some color to the room.

You Will Need

Measuring tape	Straight pins
Pillow form	Sewing machine
Fabric	Matching thread
Fabric chalk or pencil	Batting (optional)
Scissors	Needle and thread

1 Measure the pillow form (photo A); then add 1 inch to the width and height for the seam allowance. Mark the fabric (photo B) and cut the front panel of the pillow.

2 Use the front panel as a pattern to cut the material for the back of the pillow. Pin the front and back panels with right sides together.

3 Sew the seams with a straight stitch. Sew three sides of the fabric and sew in 2 inches from each corner on the fourth side. This leaves enough space to insert the pillow form.

4 Clip the corners to reduce bulk (photo C), and turn the pillow right side out. Push out the corners, and press the seams if desired.

5 Fold the pillow form and ease it into the case. If needed, add batting to the corners for a crisp look.

6 Tuck in the edges of the opening along the seam line and pin together. Sew the opening closed by hand with a blind stitch, using as small a stitch as possible.

TIPS | DIY Network Crafts

BUYING PILLOW FABRIC

When choosing the right fabric for your pillow, consider how the pillow will be used. For a pillow that will receive hard wear, select a sturdy, firmly woven fabric that will retain its shape.

7 To hide the knot at the end of hand stitching, insert the needle as for a new stitch, pull it out, and instead of pulling the thread through, wrap the thread around the needle (photo D) and pull the needle through it, creating a knot. Then, pass the needle back through the fabric to the other side of the pillow. Cut the thread close to the fabric. The tail of the thread will pull back into the pillow and be hidden.

FINISHING TOUCHES

Frame a cotton fabric print for the wall (see Fabric Wall Art, page 36), and add a canvas border to a sisal rug (see Sisal Rug Border, page 62).

TABLE MAT

Add a splash of color to the dining room or kitchen table with a simple table mat.

You Will Need

Measuring tape
Decorative fabric
Backing fabric
Sewing machine and thread
Straight pins
Iron

1 Determine the dimensions of the table mat by measuring the table length and width. Allow 10 inches of exposed table surface on all sides. Add 1 inch to the dimensions for the seam allowances on each edge. (This results in mat dimensions 18 inches less in length and width than the table measurements.)

2 Measure and mark the mat fabric according to the dimensions determined in step 1, and cut it to size. Use the decorative fabric as a pattern to cut the backing fabric.

3 Hem the backing fabric sides with a 1-inch hem. Lay the mat fabric on top of the backing with wrong sides together. Fold the decorative fabric under 1 inch on all sides, pressing if desired, and pin to the backing fabric.

4 Sew the seams by topstitching around the mat with thread in a color to subtly highlight the edges of the mat.

FRESH & HIP

Newlyweds Keith and Katie both have seamstress moms, but you wouldn't have known it by looking at their living room! They were in a brown rut and wanted a fresh new look that's current and hip.

BEFORE: Dated and drab in shades of brown, this room was comfortable but not hip and happening.

AFTER: Hand-me-down, first house furnishings become fresh and welcoming with an upholstered coffee table, throw pillows and window balance.

PROJECT SUMMARY

The Material Girls used a palette of sky blues and grassy greens to give this space a fresh, modern look. They built a coffee table, sewed a simple rod-pocket valance, and made a box cushion for the fireplace hearth.

Fabric and Color Swatches

BEFORE: Plain windows and flat, dated pillows left this room wanting.

AFTER: Earth-toned colors and comfortable textures bring this room some much-needed style. New curtains, throw pillows, and a fabric-covered coffee table combine to give the room a bold, fresh look.

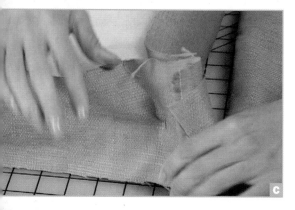

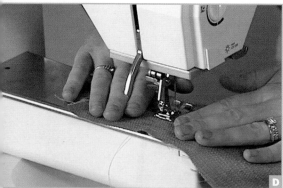

You Will Need

Foam (pre-cut)	Spray adhesive
Fabric	Straight pins
Scissors	Sewing machine and thread
Fabric chalk	Batting
Measuring tape	Fabric-covered buttons

HEARTH BOX CUSHION

1 Lay the fabric wrong side up, and position the foam onto it. If your fabric has a pattern, center the foam appropriately. Trace around the foam with chalk to create a sew line for later use. Cut away the excess fabric, leaving an inch on each side for seam allowance (photo A). Repeat for the bottom piece.

2 Measure the height of the cushion and add 2 inches for the width of the side strips. Measure the length and width of the cushion and add 2 inches to each measurement. Cut four strips according to these measurements for the sides of the cushion.

3 Spray the pre-cut foam with adhesive and wrap the batting all the way around it (photo B). Cut the excess batting at the corners to reduce bulk.

4 Pin the side strips, wrong sides out, at the corners around the foam (photo C).

5 Remove the foam and sew a straight stitch down each corner seam (photo D).

6 Slip the sides back onto the foam to make sure they fit well. Trim any excess fabric (photo E).

TIPS | DIY Network Crafts

ENSURING A TIGHT FIT
The sew line for the fabric is drawn before the batting is in place so that the cover will have a nice, tight fit with the batting included.

7 With the chalk line facing up, align the top piece with the sides (photo F), matching the corners first. Pin the seams all the way around. Remove from the foam and sew along the chalk line.

8 Repeat the process for the bottom, but leave most of one long side open to insert the foam. Turn the fabric right side out, popping out the corners as well. (See Sewing Perfect Corners, page 68)

9 Insert the foam into the cover (photo G), and pin the opening closed. Hand stitch the opening closed.

10 Using fabric chalk and a measuring tape, evenly mark where the buttons will go (photo H). Sew the buttons in place by tufting (see sidebar below).

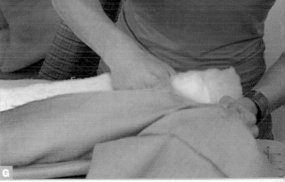

TUFTING WITH BUTTONS

Tufting creates the soft look of dimpling on fabric. To tuft with buttons, thread the needle through the top button, leaving a long tail, and push the needle through the center to the other side of the foam. Then thread the needle through the bottom button and return the needle through the foam. Tightly secure the threads together, creating a dimple in the fabric on each side.

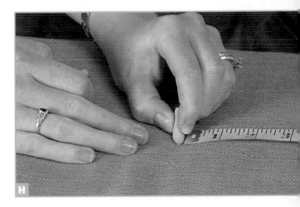

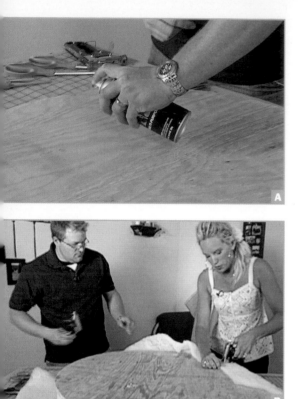

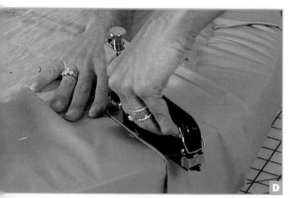

ROUND UPHOLSTERED COFFEE TABLE

Build a round coffee table out of high-density foam and batting secured to plywood. Upholster it with vinyl and fit it with wooden legs. For a decorative touch, add trim around the bottom edge of the table.

You Will Need

Foam (pre-cut to size)	Staples
Plywood (pre-cut)	Wooden legs
Spray adhesive	Drill
Vinyl fabric	Upholstery leg brackets
Scissors	Fabric for trim
Batting	Fabric glue

1 Coat the pre-cut plywood with spray adhesive (photo A). Coat the foam with spray adhesive as well and center it on top of the plywood. Press it down, making sure it is even all the way around.

2 Lay the fabric out, wrong side facing up. Lay the foam onto the fabric, plywood end up. Cut the fabric large enough to wrap around the foam and plywood. Cut the batting to the same size as the fabric.

3 Layer the batting over the wrong side of the fabric. Center the foam onto the batting, plywood side up (photo B).

4 Tightly pull the batting and staple to the bottom of the plywood, making pleats in the batting as necessary as you go (photo C).

5 Pull the fabric tightly over the batting, taking time to create neat, even pleats that run straight up and down the sides of the table. Staple into place (photo D).

6 Trim off excess fabric and add another row of staples for extra strength (photo E).

7 Attach the brackets to the bottom of the plywood with screws. Use a measuring tape to position them evenly (photo F). Then screw the legs into place on the brackets.

8 Cut a strip of fabric to the circumference of the upholstered table, plus an inch or two for overlap. Fold in the long raw edges and press. Press the raw edge in on one end as well. Determine the position for the trim (photo G), setting it to hang about ¼ inch below the bottom edge of the table.

9 Apply glue evenly to the back of the trim, over the raw edges and center, and press in place onto the table (photo H). Finish the circle with the pressed end of the strip overlapping the raw edge of the other end to cover it. Secure the end with glue.

HANGING DIVIDER PANELS

Hang these panels from the ceiling with hooks and chain to divide one room into separate spaces.

You Will Need

Fabric lining	Iron
Scissors	Straight pins
Sewing machine and thread	Hooks
Measuring tape	Chain

1 Determine the length for the panels, measuring from the floor to the height they will hang. Add 12 inches to the length for the rod pocket allowance. Add 6 inches to the desired width of your panels for seam allowances. Cut the panel fabric according to your measurements. Cut the lining to the same measurements, except subtract 6 inches from the width, to reduce bulk in sewing.

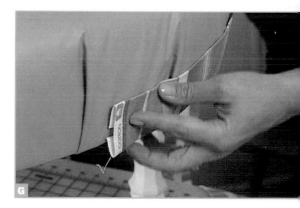

2 Fold in 3 inches on each side of the panel fabric and press. Lay the lining and the panel fabric with wrong sides together, tucking the lining under the folded edges. Turn under the raw edges of the panel for a 1½-inch hem on each side. Press and pin in place. Sew both side hems.

3 To make a rod pocket, fold the top edge of the panel fabric over 6 inches. Then, fold the raw edge under for a finished width of 3 inches. Press and pin in place. Repeat for the bottom edge. Sew both pockets.

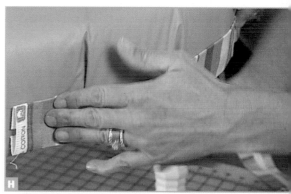

4 Insert rods in the top and bottom rod pockets, and hang the panels from the ceiling using hooks and chain.

CURTAIN ROD VALANCE

Make a simple window valance that gives the effect of a cornice board, but hangs with curtain rods on the top and bottom. Sew rod pockets on the top and bottom of the fabric, and hang.

You Will Need

Measuring tape	Iron
Fabric	Straight pins
Lining	Sewing machine and thread
Scissors	2" curtain rods
Fabric chalk	

1 Measure the width of the window to calculate the size for the valance. Add about 6 inches to allow for the valance to come out from the window at the sides. This is the length of the fabric. The finished height of the valance in this project was 10 inches. Add 4 inches to the top and bottom for the rod pocket, for a total of 18 inches for the width of the fabric.

2 Mark and cut the fabric to the dimensions determined in step 1. Repeat for the lining. With the fabric face down on the table, lay the lining face up on top of it. Fold the sides in 3 inches (photo A) and press.

3 Open the fold, and cut away the lining on the fold to make sewing easier (photo B). Fold the sides of the valance fabric in again, over the cut lining, and fold the raw edge under for a 1½-inch hem (photo C). Press to create a straight edge and pin.

4 Sew each seam with a straight stitch, hemming the sides.

5 Fold the top of the valance in 5 inches and press (photo D). Fold the raw edge under to make a 2½-inch pocket. Press the pocket and pin for sewing. Repeat for the bottom of the valance.

6 Sew a straight seam close to the inside fold of each pocket to allow as much room as possible in the pocket for the rod. Insert the curtain rods through the pockets and hang.

VARNISHED FABRIC ART

Make a simple piece of wall art using fabric, a frame, staples, and some glossy varnish. Choose a fabric with a large pattern to cut out and use as an applique for the wall art.

You Will Need

Vinyl fabric	Gloss varnish
Decorative fabric with large design	Glue
Wood frame	Small paint roller
Staple gun and staples	Scissors

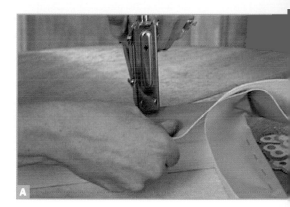

1 Cut the vinyl to size to wrap around the front and sides of the frame, reaching to the back. Secure to the back with staples (photo A). Cut off any excess vinyl.

2 Cut out shapes from the decorative fabric for the focal point of the art. Glue the cutouts to the vinyl (photo B).

3 Using the small paint roller, coat the whole piece with gloss varnish (photo C). Let dry for at least an hour.

FINISHING TOUCHES

Add decorative pillows (see Decorative Pillows, page 50) to a couch and chair, and big throw pillows for the floor. Add curtains to the windows (see Pinch Pleat Drapes, page 104). Hang two room divider panels from the ceiling to separate one room from another (see Hanging Divider Panels, page 57). In an adjoining dining room, add a coordinating tablecloth, placemats, runners for side tables (see Table Runner, page 28) and new covers for the seats.

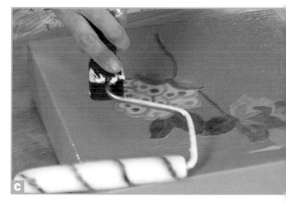

SMALL TO SPACIOUS

Newlyweds Todd and Angelique are first-time home-owners who enjoy having friends over, but their living room was small and plain. They love color and wanted to make the most of their small space to create a welcoming place for entertaining.

BEFORE: Not only drab and ordinary, this living room was also small, doubling the challenge of bringing it to life.

AFTER: Ruched pillows and a table runner add depth to the room while brightening it up.

Fabric and Color Swatches

PROJECT SUMMARY

The Material Girls used a bright palette of orange, gold, and red fabrics, plus some tricks of the trade, to design a room that feels open and spacious even in close quarters. They sewed ruched pillows, added a coordinating border to a sisal rug, and made box cushions for extra seating that tucks away under the coffee table for storage.

BEFORE: A bare kitchen pass through on a blank wall lends a sense of space to the room, but no real visual interest.

AFTER: Bright colors and a few changes like new pillows and a table runner add tons of personality. A fabric-covered cornice board over the pass through provides a visual anchor point in the once empty space.

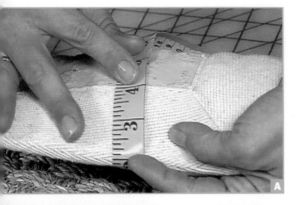

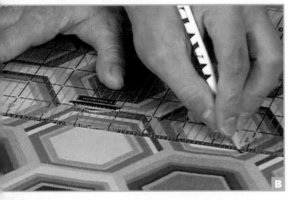

SISAL RUG BORDER

Add a little flair to a sisal rug by gluing on a new, colorful fabric border. This is a no-sew project made easy with fusible tape and fabric glue.

You Will Need	
Sisal rug	Scissors
Measuring tape	Fusible tape
Fabric	Iron
Fabric chalk	Fabric glue

1 Measure the border of the rug from front to back and add 2 inches (photo A). This is the width for cutting the new border material. Measure the length and width of the rug and add 3 inches to each measurement. These are the lengths to cut the new border material.

2 Transfer the measurements to the fabric (photo B) and cut out the new border pieces accordingly. Cut four strips—one for each edge of the rug.

3 Place a strip of fusible tape on the edge of the fabric (photo C) and fold the fabric over it, with a ½-inch fold. Press with an iron for a few seconds to activate the glue. Repeat on the other edge of the strip. Then repeat the process for each strip of fabric.

TIPS | DIY Network Crafts

MATCHING THE PATTERN
If your border fabric has an obvious pattern, make sure you fold each piece of the border the way you fold the first one, so the pattern is the same on the finished side of each border.

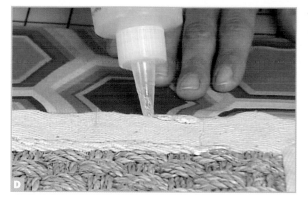

4 Leaving the corners for last, apply glue to the existing rug border. Begin gluing a few inches from the corners (photo D). Spread the glue along the edges of the rug's border and then run a squiggly line of glue down the center (photo E). Use plenty of glue so the rug can withstand vacuuming and foot traffic.

5 Using the rug border as your guide, adhere the new border strips along the top and bottom borders, and press the fabric down as you go (photo F). Then add the side strips.

6 Cut off excess fabric from one strip at each corner, cutting in from the corner to remove bulk (photo G). Add glue and wrap the remaining strip over the corner, covering the cut edge of the other strip. Fold the corner like the end of a package (photo H), using more glue as necessary to hold the material in place.

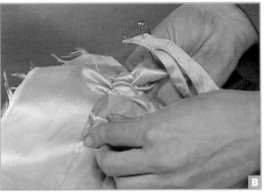

RUCHING

Ruching comes from the French word for pleat. It refers to the pleating or gathering of fabric achieved by feeding ribbon through sewn casings and then scrunching the fabric along the ribbon before sewing the pillow sides together.

◀ RUCHED PILLOWS ▶

These pillows are made in elongated styles to visually lengthen a couch or love seat. Make the luxurious gathers of the pillows by sewing casings and running ribbons through them. After you sew and stuff the pillow, you'll tie the ruching ribbon into decorative bows.

You Will Need

Fabric	Straight pins
Measuring tape	Sewing machine
Lining	Ribbon
Scissors	Safety pins
Fabric chalk	Polyester fiberfill

1 Determine the size for the pillow, adding 1 inch to each dimension for seam allowance.

2 Cut out the back piece of fabric to those measurements. For the front piece, double the length to allow for the ruching and cut. Or, add more fabric for greater effect with the gathers. Cut out two pieces of lining the same size as the fabric pieces.

3 To make the casing, measure 2½ inches from the edge of the wrong side of the top piece of fabric. Mark a straight line across the fabric with fabric chalk. Measure in one more inch, and mark another line (photo A). Repeat this process on the other edge of the fabric.

4 Pin the fabric and lining pieces together, and sew along the marked lines on each side to create the ribbon casings.

5 Cut a piece of ribbon to the length of the top piece of fabric. Secure a safety pin on each end of the ribbon. Pin one end to the top of the fabric; feed the other end through the casing (photo B). Repeat for the second casing.

6 Use the ribbons like a drawstring, bunching the fabric along the ribbon to create the ruching. Work the gathers evenly (photo C). Adjust the ruching so the length of the front piece matches the length of the back piece.

7 Along the casing opening, measure in 1½ inches from the edge and cut a small slit in the right side of the pillow within the casing to pull the end of the ribbon through (photo D). Repeat for each end of the ribbon. Then pin the ribbon ends to the top of the fabric to keep it from shifting while sewing.

8 Lay the back and front pieces with right sides together. Pin the edges, holding the gathers in place with as many pins as necessary (photo E).

9 Sew the pieces together with a straight stitch, pivoting at each corner. Leave one side seam open between the casings to turn the pillow right side out.

10 Remove all of the pins, turn the pillow right side out, and pop out the corners.

11 Unpin the ribbons, knot them, and tie bows on all four corners (photo F).

12 Stuff the pillow with polyester fiberfill (photo G). Then, pin the opening closed and hand stitch securely. Remove the pins.

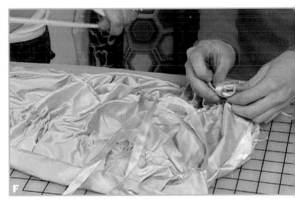

TIPS | DIY Network Crafts

FEEDING RIBBON THROUGH CASING

Be sure to distribute extra fabric down the length of the ribbon as you push the safety pin through. Too much fabric bunching will make it harder to work the pin through the casing.

MAKING SMALL SPACES BIGGER

Try these ideas to add a sense of space to a small room.

Choosing Fabrics

Don't be afraid of big patterns like a large-scale floral fabric in a small room. Just make sure the other fabrics are smaller prints, solids, or softer tone-on-tone styles.

Pillow Overload

Too many pillows can overwhelm a small space, so use fewer pillows in elongated styles, such as the ruched pillows in this project. Or use other long, narrow pillows.

Room to Room

Another way to make the most of a small space is to tie it visually to an adjoining room—use fabrics from the living room as accents in an open kitchen, for instance.

Wall Art

A large piece of wall art can also increase the sense of space in a small room. A horizontal pattern will draw the eye horizontally across the wall, making the wall seem longer.

Window Illusion

Give one window on a wall the appearance of several with a long curtain rod and a few extra fabric panels.

◄ CUSHION OTTOMAN ►

This boxy cushion is great for extra seating and can be stored under a coffee table to conserve space when not in use. A plywood base gives it bottom support and structure. Simply glue high-density foam to the wood base, and sew a fabric slipcover to dress it. For a professional finish, add a bottom piece of fabric underneath the ottoman to cover the staple seams.

You Will Need

Foam (pre-cut)	Scissors
Plywood (pre-cut)	Straight pins
Spray adhesive	Sewing machine and thread
Measuring tape	Staple gun and staples
Fabric	Fabric glue

1 Determine the size for the ottoman, taking into account the space under your coffee table, if applicable, for storing. Have a cube of foam cut to size when you purchase it at a local foam store. Have the plywood pre-cut as well, or use a jigsaw to cut it to the size of the foam.

2 Spray the plywood with adhesive and center the foam in place, pressing to adhere it (photo A). The plywood will give stability to the foam.

3 Cut the top piece of the fabric to the size of the foam, plus 1 inch to length and width for the seam allowance. For the side pieces add 1 inch to the width of the foam, and several inches to the length for stapling underneath the ottoman. Cut a piece of fabric for the bottom as well, but subtract 2 inches from the length and width of the top piece.

4 Pin all four side pieces, with right sides together, like a box. Slip the fabric over the foam to make sure it fits, if desired, and finish pinning.

5 Sew all four seams with a straight stitch and ½-inch seam allowance.

6 Fit the sewn sides over the foam (leaving the wrong sides facing out) and pin the top piece to the edges, with right sides together. Pin all four corners first (photo B). Then pin the middle, setting pins close together and easing the fabric between each corner for a clean fit.

7 Remove the fabric from the foam, and sew the top piece onto the side pieces. (See sidebar, Sewing Perfect Corners, page 68.)

TIPS | DIY Network Crafts

◢ NO FRAYED EDGES
Use pinking shears to cut the edges of the bottom piece of the ottoman to prevent the fabric from fraying since it will not be hemmed.

◢ LABEL FABRIC PIECES
When working with a number of pieces of fabric of similar sizes, as in this project, label them on the wrong side with fabric chalk or tape to prevent having to remeasure each piece if they are mixed up (photo below).

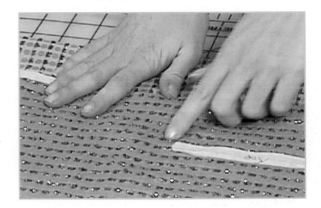

8 Turn the fabric right side out, popping out the corners as well. Gently ease the fabric over the ottoman (photo C).

9 Fasten the edges of the fabric to the plywood with a staple gun (photo D), beginning in the middle of each side and saving the corners for last. Pull the fabric snug without overstretching, keeping the fabric pattern aligned.

10 At the corners, fold the fabric like a package so it will lay flat, and staple it in place. Trim any excess fabric.

11 Evenly cover the wrong side of the bottom piece of fabric with fabric glue (photo E). Position over the bottom side of the ottoman to cover the staples (photo F), and press into place.

SEWING PERFECT CORNERS

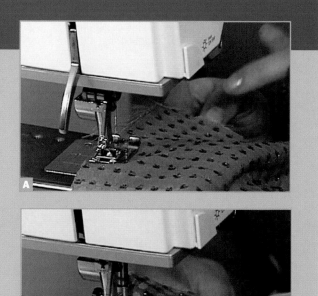

1 With fabric pinned together, begin sewing along one side edge a few inches up from the corner (photo A).

2 Stop the machine ½ inch from the edge, leaving the needle down in the fabric.

3 Lift the presser foot and pivot the fabric (photo B).

4 Put the presser foot down and continue sewing the next side.

Repeat at each corner. (If necessary, to turn the fabric right side out, as for a pillow case, leave a gap in the middle of the last seam.)

5 Clip the seam allowance at each corner for a smooth look when you turn the fabric right side out. Turn the fabric and use a chopstick or eraser-end of a pencil to gently push out the corners if necessary.

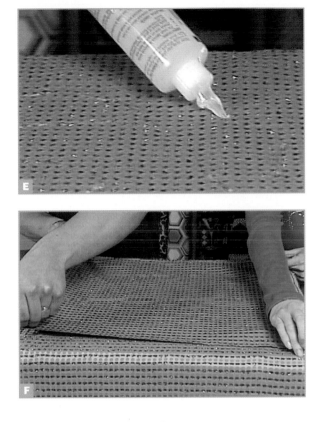

FINISHING TOUCHES

Add decorative pillows to couches (see Pieced Designer Pillow, page 37; Tufted Round Pillow, page 36; Decorative Pillows, page 50). A long wall of curtains gives the illusion of a larger room (see Pinch Pleat Drapes, page 104), and a runner (see Table Runner, page 28) can add a splash of color to a coffee table. Add a fabric-covered cornice board (see Curtain Rod Valance, page 58) to give interest to the kitchen pass through, and a reversible runner (see Table Runner, page 28) to change with the mood.

3

Kids' Rooms

Create a space that's suited just for your child—from newborn to teen—with color, creativity, and convenience in mind too. From giant foam building blocks that you can sew to the ultimate chill lounge for a teen's room, this chapter is brimming with ideas to bring back your own youthful spirit and design a room that will reflect your child's unique personality.

PLAY ZONE CENTRAL

Cristin and Cory finished the walls and floors of their basement to create a playroom for their three young boys, but that's as far as they got. It's a big open space with no color, no style, and no organization. They need some help to make it into a fun play space for the boys.

BEFORE: Lacking color, order, and warmth, this basement was no fun for young children.

AFTER: Colorful and full of soft building blocks and new felt boards, this room is a toddler's paradise.

AFTER: Fun pillows and new curtains make the space a relaxing spot for mom and dad to spend time with their three boys.

Fabric and Color Swatches

PROJECT SUMMARY

The Material Girls selected fabrics in red, blue, and tan and came up with some ideas for organizing this space—and, most importantly, the toys. They used fabric to infuse color and create play zones in the room, making tack-less bulletin boards, tab top curtains, and soft, giant building blocks out of foam.

AFTER: Framed pictures of the kids and a fresh coat of paint continue the design and color theme to another wall in the room.

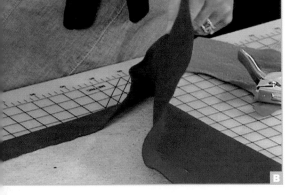

FELT-COVERED BOARDS

Cover pieces of fiber board with felt to create felt boards. Then cut shapes of every kind in felt for kids to stick to the board--no tacks needed! Felt sticks to felt because of static cling.

You Will Need

24" x 36" fiber board	Drill or screwdriver
30" x 42" felt	Felt squares or scraps, various colors
Staple gun	Stencils or patterns for shapes
Scissors	
Wall anchors and screws	Tacky glue or hot glue gun

1 Center the fiber board on one piece of felt. Wrap the felt to the back of the board tightly and place a staple at the center of each side of the board (photo A).

2 Make sure the felt is distributed evenly and tightly. Continue stapling around all sides of the board, staying several inches from the corners--leaving them for last (photo B).

TIPS | DIY Network Crafts

RIGHT SIDE UP

Felt is a great fabric to work with because it has no wrong or right side. No need to worry which side is up!

TIPS | DIY Network Crafts

FIBER BOARD

Fiber board is made out of recycled paper. It's lightweight, easy to work with, and can be cut with a utility knife. Buy it at your local building or lumber supply store.

3 Miter the corners for a smooth finish (see sidebar).

4 Attach the felt boards to the wall using wall anchors and screws. To cover the wall anchors that attach to the board, glue small pieces of felt to the board with tacky glue (photo C).

5 Use stencils to trace images onto various colors of felt, or make patterns from computer printouts of animals, letters, numbers, or other objects. Cut out the pieces, and accent them with cutouts of contrasting colors applied with glue (photo D).

MITERED CORNERS

To make the cleanest corners possible for the boards, miter them.

1 Fold the corner of the material in toward the board (photo A). Then fold one side over the middle (photo B) and staple.

2 Trim away excess felt, if desired. Fold down the felt that remains and staple in place to finish the miter (photo C).

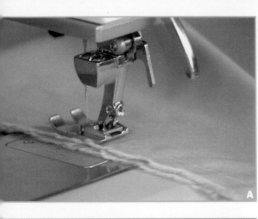

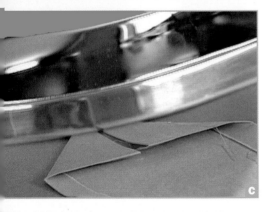

CURTAINS WITH TABS & BUTTONS

Make tab-topped curtains for the window in the playroom, pressing and tacking simple fabric strips at the top of the material. Add a facing to the top of the curtain, and buttons and rickrack trim as accents.

You Will Need

Fabric	Straight pins
Measuring tape	Hand-sewing needle and thread
Scissors	Buttons
Sewing machine and thread	Rickrack trim

1 Decide on the finished length of the curtain panels (see sidebar Measuring for Curtains, page 115, being sure to allow for the hem and top seam allowance, about 10 inches. These curtains were made at 1½ fullness. Cut the fabric to size for panels.

2 Pin the panels with right sides together, and sew them using a ½-inch seam allowance (photo A).

3 Fold and press the side hems, turning under 1½ inches twice. Fold and press the bottom hem, turning under 4 inches twice. Sew the sides and hem.

4 Depending on the size of the rod, cut the tabs about 12 inches long and 6 inches wide.

5 With the wrong side up, press under ¼ inch on three sides of the tab, leaving one narrow end unpressed (photo B).

6 Fold the corners of the pressed end together into a point and press (photo C).

7 Fold both long sides to the center and press (photo D).

8 Tack the corners together by hand with a needle and thread.

9 Lay the tabs on the front of the curtain panel with right sides facing up. Use a measuring tape to space them evenly apart (photo E), and pin in place.

10 Machine baste the tabs to the panel using a long stitch.

11 Sew a facing by cutting a strip of fabric about 12 inches wide and as long as the width of the curtain, adding 3 inches on each narrow end for a seam allowance.

12 Press under 1½ inches twice on each narrow end. Sew the fold in place.

13 Fold the facing in half along the length with wrong sides together and press.

14 Lay the facing along the top of the curtain, over the basted tabs, with raw edges even (photo F). Pin in place. Sew with a ½-inch seam allowance.

15 Open the facing seam and press (photo G). Then, turn the facing to the other side of the curtain and press again.

16 Use a measuring tape to fold each tab to the same height. Position a button on the pointed end of each tab (photo H). Sew the buttons to the curtain, sewing through all layers of fabric, and holding the tabs in place.

17 Machine stitch rick-rack to the curtain for an additional accent.

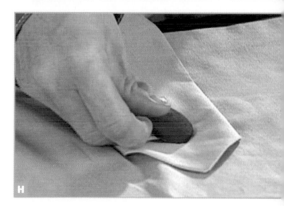

TIPS | DIY Network Crafts

ROOM TO WORK
Use a large surface, such as a dining room table, to make the job of cutting panels of curtain fabric easier.

GIANT FOAM BUILDING BLOCKS

Sew bright colors of microfiber fabric into durable covers for foam blocks in this project. Make the covers with one strip of fabric to wrap the block and two side pieces sewn in. Use hook-and-loop tape for closures so the covers can be easily removed and washed.

You Will Need

5"-thick foam squares and rectangles (pre-cut)	Scissors
Measuring tape	Sewing machine and thread
Fabric (assorted colors)	Hook-and-loop tape

1 Measure around the circumference of the foam block (photo A), and add 2 inches for seams and overlap. Then, measure the length and add 1 inch for seam allowances. Cut one piece of fabric to these measurements for the center piece.

2 For the end pieces, measure the height and width of one end of the block, adding 1 inch to each measurement for seam allowances. Cut two pieces of fabric to these measurements.

3 Pin the hook-and-loop tape to the center piece of fabric, tucking the raw edge of the fabric under the tape (photo B). Pin one side of the tape to one end of the material on the right side; pin the other side of the tape to the other end of the material on the wrong side. Machine stitch the tape securely in place.

4 Lay one small side piece at the end of the long center piece with the right sides together, matching the corners. Make a small snip on the center fabric to mark the length of the side piece (photo C). Then slide the side piece to the other side of the snip (photo D), and pin it in place for sewing.

5 Sew the length of one end of the side piece to the center piece (photo E), stopping before the corner.

6 Clip the corner with scissors to make it easier to turn the fabric for the next seam (photo F).

7 Sew to the corner, leave the needle down in the fabric, turn the fabric 90 degrees, and align the bottom fabric with the top fabric again to sew the next seam.

8 Repeat steps 5 through 7 for the next two sides. Stop sewing just before the hook-and-loop tape.

9 Align the hook-and-loop tape and secure. Then, continue sewing the seam, sewing over the tape and finishing the remaining side.

10 Repeat steps 4 through 9 to sew the other side panel onto the center panel, opening the hook-and-loop tape for ease in sewing, until repeating step 9.

11 Turn the cover right side out. Stuff the foam block into the cover, making sure to match the corners, and align the hook-and-loop tape to seal.

TIPS | DIY Network Crafts

FINDING FOAM
Check with your local upholstery supplier for foam for this project. Ask to have the squares and rectangles pre-cut for you at the store.

FINISHING TOUCHES

Make a custom cushion to cover a toy box (see Hearth Box Cushion, page 54), and polka-dot pillows to accent a sofa and chair (see Decorative Pillows, page 50).

STYLIN' PAD
WITH CHILL LOUNGE

Lucky high school freshman Vera earned the rite-of-passage to move from her small bedroom into the family's spacious bonus room. But the bland colors and barren basement walls were not inspiring for this young artist. She needed some help turning her space into a creative, stylish pad.

BEFORE: This finished basement had a large window for light, but the room was still cold and unimaginative.

AFTER: Wall panels create an artistic focal point on the wall and bolster pillows add form and softness.

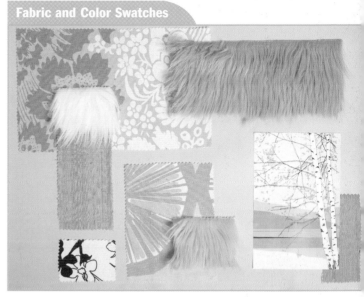

Fabric and Color Swatches

PROJECT SUMMARY

Working off of Vera's creativity, bohemian style, and love of color, the Material Girls used blues and greens paired with some fun textures and prints. They made a bolster pillow, faux fur throw rugs, fun and colorful wall art with fabric and paint, and custom wall panels to make a stylish teen pad and turn a basement alcove into the ultimate chill lounge.

AFTER: Plenty of throw pillows and fabric art she detailed herself make a signature room for this teen.

AFTER: Curtains, cushions and awesome pillows turn this basement nook into the ultimate chill lounge.

BOLSTER PILLOW

Make a bolster pillow, covering foam with a fabric case. Use lining around the foam so the bolster will be easy to insert and remove from the casing, and to make cleaning easy, use hook-and-loop tape to secure the pillow case.

You Will Need

Bolster foam form (pre-cut)	Spray adhesive
Measuring Tape	Fabric
Lining	Sewing machine and thread
Pencil	Straight pins
Scissors	Hook-and-loop tape

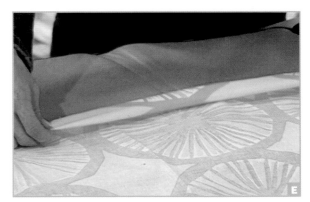

1 Measure around the circumference of the pillow form (photo A) and add 3 inches. Then measure the length of the pillow form. Using these measurements, cut the lining to size.

2 For end pieces for the lining, trace one end of the bolster onto the lining fabric (photo B). Double the lining fabric, and cut out both end pieces at once.

3 Spray adhesive onto the foam bolster (photo C), and press the center piece of the lining in place first.

4 Glue on the end pieces in the same way, and trim any excess fabric (photo D).

5 To cut out the fabric for the cover, begin with the measurements used for the lining and add 1 inch to the width and ½ inch to each end piece for seam allowances.

6 On one long side of the center piece, fold the fabric over 1½ inches. Then tuck the raw edge under ½ inch and press (photo E). Do the same for the other long edge of the center piece.

7 Cut the hook-and-loop tape to the length of the bolster, minus 4 inches. Align the tape 2 inches from each end on one of the long sides just pressed (photo F). Pin in place.

8 On the opposite pressed side, place the hook-and-loop tape on the right side of the fabric. Position 2 inches from each end, and pin in place (photo G).

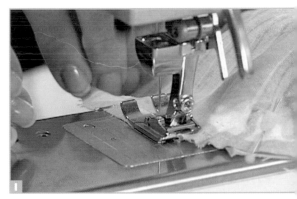

9 Sew the tape in place, beginning by backstitching the tape to the fabric and then sewing as close to the edge as possible (photo H) on both edges of the tape. Repeat for the other piece of tape. Be sure to backstitch on all of the ends so the tape is well secured.

10 Remove all of the pins. Turn the fabric inside out, and close the hook and loop tape.

11 Line up one end piece on the bolster cover with right sides together. Pin the pieces in place, and sew together (photo I). Clip the seam allowance a few times as you sew to ease the fabric together. Repeat for the other end piece.

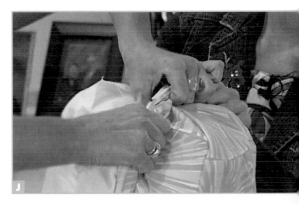

12 Remove the pins, and turn the pillowcase inside out. Insert the pillow form (photo J) and close, pressing the hook-and-loop tape together.

WALL PANELS

Make upholstered wall panels to pad the walls of an alcove. Using fabric, foam, and wood, create the perfect accessory to add contrast, texture, and softness to bare walls.

You Will Need

Plywood, cut to desired size	Pencil
Foam	Stud finder
Utility knife or electric carving knife	Drill
Measuring tape	Screws
Spray adhesive	Wood trim, mitered and painted
Scissors	Nail gun
Fabric	Finishing nails
Staple gun and staples	Caulk

A

TIPS | DIY Network Crafts

STRAIGHT EDGE
Make sure the foam is cut with a very straight edge, since it will be the border of the fabric panel.

1 Use a utility knife or electric carving knife to cut a piece of foam to the size of the plywood, less the width of the wood trim you will use.

2 Spray the plywood with adhesive (photo A) and center the foam onto the board, pressing in place.

3 Lay the fabric face up on top of the foam, and make sure that any pattern is centered. Pull the fabric snugly, but not so tightly that it stretches out of shape.

4 Staple the fabric to the plywood, stapling right up against the foam (photo B). Start at the center of one side, and set in several staples to hold the material. Then, continue stapling, smoothing the fabric as you go. Move to the opposite side of the board to help keep the fabric centered. Then finish the other sides, starting in the center and working toward the corners.

5 To hang the panel, measure and mark the center top with pencil. Also mark the center of the wall. Use a stud finder to locate the studs along the wall and mark them.

6 Measure the desired height for the panel from the ceiling down. Position the panel on the wall according to the measurements.

7 Attach the top of the panel using screws driven into the wall studs (photo C). At the bottom, use the stud finder and finish inserting the screws into the wall studs (photo D).

8 Attach the wood trim along the edges with a nail gun and finishing nails (photo E). Add caulk to the corners and to mask the finishing nails for a final touch.

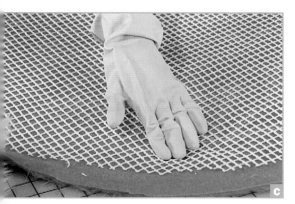

FAUX FUR RUGS

Make throw rugs out of bright colors of faux fur as a simple way to add a little texture and splash of color to a bland floor.

You Will Need

Faux fur	Non-slip rug mesh
Measuring tape	Straight pins
String	Spray adhesive
Pencil	Rubber gloves
Scissors	

1 Determine the diameter for your circular rug and divide in half for the radius.

2 Fold the fabric in half with right sides together. Pin a string to the fold at the center of the fabric. Measure down the string the length of the radius determined in step 1, and draw a half circle all the way around the fabric (photo A).

3 Cut through both layers of fabric along the line drawn. When you reach the halfway point, move to the opposite side and finish cutting the circle. Pull off any loose fur (photo B).

4 Repeat steps 2 and 3 with the mesh backing, but make the circle smaller to keep the edges of the fur from getting into the mesh.

5 Spray adhesive on the back of the rug. Wearing rubber gloves, press the mesh to the back of the faux fur (photo C). Let the adhesive dry for 10 to 20 minutes before placing the rug on the floor.

TIPS | DIY Network Crafts

MIXING AND LAYERING

Great design is all about the details, so to add color and interest, mix and layer your fabrics as you add finishing touches to the room.

PAINTED FABRIC WALL ART

Make fabric art by using black and white patterned fabric, canvas frames, and bright acrylic paints.

You Will Need

Canvas frame	Acrylic paints
Fabric	Paint brushes
Staple gun and staples	

1 Lay the fabric face down on the table and center the canvas frame on the fabric.

2 Using the staple gun, secure the fabric to the canvas frame (photo A). Start in the middle and work out toward the edges. Pull opposite sides tight and staple them in place.

3 Repeat step 2 for the remaining two sides. Leave the corners for last. Then, finish them using a mitering technique (photo B).

4 Use acrylic paints and paint brushes to paint and embellish the fabric as desired (photo C).

FINISHING TOUCHES

Sew a comforter and pillow shams (see Flanged Pillow Sham, page 32), and add accents with more throw pillows for the bed (see Decorative Pillows, page 50). Hang a curtain behind the bed that doubles as a piece of art (see Pinch Pleat Drapes, page 104). Add curtains to an alcove (see Reversible Curtains, page 114) and a valance to a basement window (see Valance, page 58) to add balance. Mix and layer fabrics and textures with table runners (see Table Runner, page 28 and Table Matte, page 51) to add interest.

BABY'S NURSERY

Todd and Joann had one boy, one girl, and a new house decorated to fit. Then along came the surprise of baby number three! They needed help to transform a guest bedroom into a nursery.

BEFORE: This guest room was a blank slate just waiting for a plan.

AFTER: A colorful frog-themed bumper pad adds interest and charm and two shelves with fabric backing become storybook-like with small fabric-covered rooftops.

Fabric and Color Swatches

▓ PROJECT SUMMARY ▓

The Material Girls created a unique red-and-black color theme for the nursery with an adorable accent of green frogs. They turned a desk into a changing table with a portable changing top and a table skirt, made a custom bumper pad, and created wall art to decorate the new nursery.

AFTER: A bed skirt gives the crib color and depth.

AFTER: Valance-topped plaid curtains complete the nursery's look.

▶ CHANGING TABLE SKIRT ◀

Transform a desk into a changing table by sewing a table skirt out of striped fabric and some elastic.

You Will Need

Desk or table	Sewing machine and thread
Measuring tape	Iron
Fabric	Safety pins
Scissors	Elastic
Straight pins	

1 Measure just under the desktop to the floor (photo A). Add 2 inches for the seam allowance and an additional 3 inches for the elastic (or adjust according to the size of your elastic). This will be the length of the fabric.

2 Next measure around the desk (photo B). Multiply the desk measurement by 1½ for fullness—or adjust to your desired fullness. Add ⅝ inch for each seam allowance.

3 Cut the fabric panels to size and place the right sides together. Make sure to match up the pattern if the fabric has one (see Matching Fabric Pattern, page 44).

4 Pin two panels together at the selvage. Sew with a straight machine stitch. Repeat until all of the panels are sewn together, including the last seam, creating a circle of fabric (photo C). Press the seams open flat.

5 To create the bottom hem, fold the fabric under 2 inches (photo D); then fold the raw edge under again. Press to make a cleaner fold, checking the hem width as you go to keep it even (photo E). Then, pin and stitch into place (photo F).

6 Use the same process as the bottom hem to make the casing for the elastic. For a 1 inch casing, fold in 2 inches of fabric. Then fold the raw edge under 1 inch (photo G).

7 Press, pin, and sew in place. Leave an opening at least 2½ times the width of the elastic for inserting the elastic.

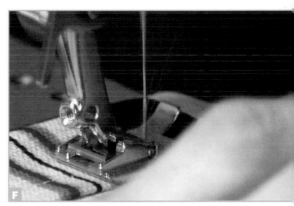

TIPS | DIY Network Crafts

ELASTIC CASING

Elastic comes in different sizes so make sure that the casing you sew is large enough for the elastic to fit inside, but not so large that the elastic will twist around in the casing.

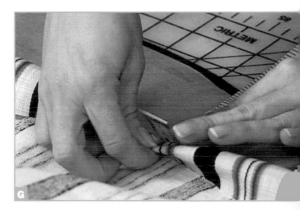

8 Secure a safety pin on each end of the elastic. Fasten one end of the elastic to the skirt just outside the casing opening. Feed the loose end with a safety pin into the casing, making sure that the elastic does not twist inside (photo H).

9 Work the pin all the way around the skirt inside the casing. Bring it back out the opening and hold it securely for the next step.

10 Place the skirt around the table. Pull the elastic until the skirt cinches to the appropriate size (photo I). Pin the elastic together to keep the skirt cinched.

11 Remove the skirt from the table and machine sew back and forth over the elastic to secure it (photo J). Cut off any excess elastic, and hand stitch the opening closed (see Closing a Gap with Hand Stitching, page 97).

12 Fit the skirt over the desk and even out the gathers (photo K).

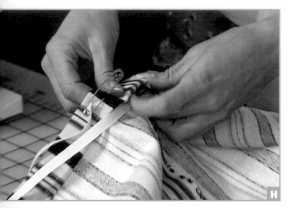

PORTABLE CHANGING TRAY

Build a portable top for a changing table out of wood and fabric, and add a compartment for holding diapers, baby powder, and wipes. Size this changing tray to fit your table or desk.

You Will Need

1" x 4" boards	Screws
Plywood	Foam changing pad
Measuring tape	Pen
Nail gun	Fabric
Drill	Staple gun

1 Measure the size of the table and cut the plywood and 1 x 4s accordingly. Include four pieces of 1 x 4 to frame the tray and one piece for a divider.

2 Use a nail gun to build the frame with 1 x 4s (photo A). Set the divider aside until step 4.

3 To create the base, set the plywood over the assembled frame. Drill screw holes through the plywood and just into the frame below. Drill one screw hole at each corner, and two along each edge (photo B). Then secure the base to the frame with screws.

4 Flip the tray over and insert the foam changing pad to determine where the divider will go. Slide the divider next to the changing pad and measure the distance from the divider to the side (photo C). Set the divider aside.

5 Remove the changing pad and flip the tray back over. Measure and mark the distance determined in step 4 on the bottom. Pre-drill holes for the divider all the way through the base (photo D).

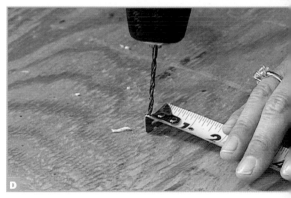

CAREFUL CUTTING

When upholstering, always be careful of how much excess fabric you cut as you are mitering corners or trimming other areas. Cut conservatively first; then cut again if needed.

6 Set the divider in the tray, and using the holes as a guide, mark the location for the screws onto the divider (photo E). Pre-drill the holes in the divider and set it aside.

7 Lay the fabric out on the frame, smoothing and contouring as you go. The fabric will wrap around the inside of the tray and outside to the bottom, so be sure you have enough fabric for all four sides (photo F).

8 Fold one edge of fabric under to create a hem, and anchor it in place on the bottom plywood with a few staples in the center (photo G). Tuck under the rest of the hem along the side and secure with staples.

9 Turn the tray over, and note where the divider will go. Pull the fabric tight and staple it along the inside edges of the tray (photo H). Continue on the opposite side of the tray, smoothing out the bottom. Pull the fabric tightly to keep it straight. Secure with staples.

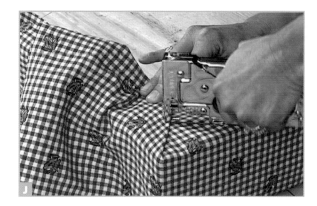

10 Flip the tray over again to finish stapling the fabric to the long sides of the plywood (photo I).

11 At the ends, secure a few staples in the center. Miter the corner on one side and secure with a staple. Tuck and trim the excess fabric from the other side until the corner looks smooth. Miter and staple (photo J).

12 Cover the divider with fabric. Make sure that the wood is lined up straight on the fabric. Then fold the raw edges in on the end to create a clean hem (photo K). Wrap the fabric around the wood, noting the placement of the pre-drilled holes. Cut a dart in the edge of the fabric at each hole (photo L).

13 Staple the fabric along the edge of the board, being careful not to staple where the screws will go (photo M). Pull the other side tightly around the wood, cut darts for the screw holes, and secure the fabric with staples.

14 Working on the bottom of the tray, slowly drive each screw into a pre-drilled hole, until it just pokes through on the fabric. Set the divider in place in the frame on the screw tips, hold firmly, and drive the screws through the pre-drilled holes in the divider (photo N).

15 Add the changing pad, and set the changing tray in place on the table.

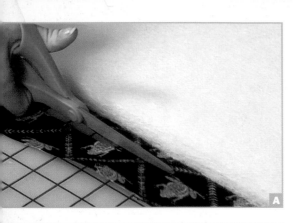

BUMPER PAD

Make a bumper pad for a crib using bumper pad inserts or batting and cover them with fabric. Tie ribbons to secure the pad to the crib.

You Will Need

Fabric	Straight pins
Batting or bumper pad inserts	Ribbon
Scissors	Needle and thread
Sewing machine and thread	

1 Using the pre-cut batting as a guide, cut out two fabric panels for each pad, adding about 1/2 inch on each side for seam allowance (photo A).

2 Pin the pieces together with the right sides facing. Make sure the pattern on the fabric matches (see Matching the Fabric Pattern, page 44).

3 Sew the panels together with a straight stitch, leaving an opening to insert the bumper pad. Notch the seam allowance of each corner before turning the fabric right side out (photo B).

4 Turn the fabric right side out and insert the batting. To finish, tuck under the raw edges and hand stitch the opening closed (see sidebar, opposite page).

5 To add ties to each corner, cut four lengths of ribbon about 24 inches. Or, adjust the measurement based on the size of the slats on the crib.

TIPS | DIY Network Crafts

JUMPING FROGS

If you use a directional fabric like this one with green jumping frogs, be sure to sew all of the panels with the frogs jumping the same direction—out of the crib!

SEWING CRISP CORNERS

When sewing the corner of a seam, stop with the needle down in the fabric at the corner. Lift the presser foot and turn the fabric 90 degrees, in position to sew the next side. Put the presser foot back down, and continue sewing. This gives a square, crisp corner to the seam.

6 Fold the ribbons in half over the corner of the bumper pad (photo C), making sure they are even on both sides. Machine stitch the folded edge of the ribbon in place over the corner of the bumper pad.

FINISHING TOUCHES

Make wall art with wooden letters, fabric, and glue. Add curtains to the windows (see page 44), pillows (see page 50) and a bed skirt (see page 90) to the crib, and fabric backs on the bookcases (see page 116). Top off each bookcase with little plywood rooftops covered with fabric.

CLOSING A GAP WITH HAND STITCHING

Many projects call for sewing fabric together inside out and leaving a gap in the seam to turn the fabric. When the fabric is turned out and you are ready to sew up the gap, here's a good technique for a finished look.

1 Thread a hand-sewing needle and knot the end of the thread. Insert the needle from the inside of the seam to hide the knot and pull out to the outside of the fabric.

2 Take the needle across the opening to the outside of the fabric. Thinking of the opening as a tunnel, keep your stitches close together on the outside, but make your progress in the tunnel.

3 Insert the needle into the fabric right across from where you first inserted it. Then, angle the needle in the tunnel to bring it out of the fabric further down.

4 Enter the fabric for the next stitch close to the first, again angling it in the tunnel to bring it out of the fabric further down.

5 Tie a knot at the end of the seam, looping the needle through an existing stitch and then knotting through the loop of thread from the needle. Or, insert the needle into the seam, bringing it out elsewhere on the fabric. Pull the thread taut and clip close to the fabric without knotting. When the fabric pulls back to shape, the loose end of the thread will be pulled inside and hidden.

4

Work Rooms

This chapter is your source for ideas for all of the productive rooms of the house—from the kitchen to the study to the home office. Soften too-sterile walls, shelves, desks, and tables with accents and amendments that will make your work a pleasure, and create a comfortable surrounding that's efficient and practical too. The projects on these pages will help you get the job done.

HOME OFFICE COMFORTS

A career change for Jim meant that he could work from home; he only needed an office space that would allow him a bit of privacy in his busy household. He needed help deciding what should stay from the old office and what should go, and how to turn the room into an efficient, inviting place to do business.

BEFORE: All utilitarian, this office space needed some personality to be a welcoming place to work.

Fabric and Color Swatches

PROJECT SUMMARY

The Material Girls created a masculine and very functional home office that is both professional and homey for this family. They built a bench to connect standard shelving and added extra seating, a faux leather desk top, and pinch pleat drapes for color and smart style on the window.

AFTER: A cozy bench tucked between shelves adds texture, color and softness— as well as extra seating and bonus storage below.

◁ PADDED BENCH ▷

Construct this bench of 2 x 4s and plywood; then cover it with batting and fabric to suit your office space. This bench was used to connect standard shelving and add extra seating. Add a skirt to the bench to provide additional storage underneath as well.

You Will Need

Four 2 x 4s (pre-cut to desired length)	Spray adhesive
Drill	Batting
3" screws	Fabric
2½" screws	Staple gun and staples
¾" plywood (2 pieces pre-cut to desired length)	Metal brackets
3" to 4" foam	Furniture legs

1 Lay out the frame of the bench with the 2 x 4s (photo A). Pre-drill holes and use 3-inch screws to attach the boards. Use two screws at each joint for strength.

2 Position one piece of plywood over the frame. Pre-drill holes at the edges along the sides of the frame. Using 2½-inch screws, attach the plywood to the frame (photo B). Repeat on the other side of the frame to create the bottom.

3 Spray adhesive over the top of the plywood and the bottom of the foam with long, even strokes. Position the foam on top of the plywood, with equal overhang on each side (photo C), and press it into place. The overhang provides softness to the edge of the bench.

TIPS | DIY Network Crafts

ATTACHING PLYWOOD TO FRAME
When attaching the screws to hold the plywood in place, take care not to secure them over the joints of the frame, where you may run into screws from the frame.

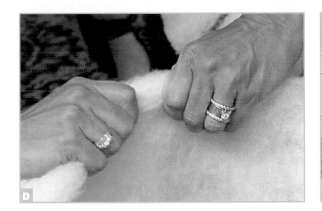

4 Cut the batting to fit over the foam top and sides of the bench. Add an inch or two to the original size of the bench to allow for overlap. Also cut the fabric, adding 10 extra inches to make sure it will fit over the foam and batting.

5 Lay the batting out on the floor. Center the bench on top of the batting, foam side down.

6 Sit on the bottom of the bench while you pull the batting tightly around the sides. Your body weight helps insure a tight fit and helps round out the sides of the bench cushion. Staple the batting in place, starting in the center, working outward, and alternating sides. Set staples 1 inch apart, leaving the corners for last.

7 Miter the batting at the corners, cutting or simply tearing off the excess (photo D). Tuck the edge under and staple it down for a smooth finish (photo E).

8 Repeat steps 5 through 7 with the fabric. At the corners, pull the fabric tight (photo F), fold, and anchor it with a staple at the corner. Tuck under the excess and staple (photo G). Continue folding and stapling to make the corner as flat as possible.

9 Install the metal brackets for the legs with screws, positioning them 1 inch in from the edges (photo H), and screw the legs into position.

ADDING A BENCH SKIRT

For a more decorative look, purchase additional fabric to add a skirt to the bench. Create one skirt panel for the front and one for each side to give easy access to storage underneath. In this case, the bench was against the wall so a back panel was not needed.

You Will Need

Fabric	Iron
Scissors	Pressing cloth
Measuring tape	Tacking strip
Fusible tape	Staple gun and staples

1 Follow steps 1 through 3 of Bookcase Curtains (page 117), making one panel for the front of the bench and one for each side. (If the bench sits against the wall, a panel is not needed for the back.)

2 To attach the panels to the bench, turn the bench upside down, and lay a skirt panel in place, right sides together, along the edge of the bench bottom.

3 Position a tacking strip on top of the material and staple both in place along the edge of the bottom. Repeat for additional panels of the skirt.

PINCH PLEAT DRAPES AND VALANCE

Make these simple drapery panels and add decorative pinch pleats along the top for extra volume and a tailored look. A coordinating valance ties the whole piece together. The curtain rods in this project were longer than the opening of the window to give the sense of a larger window.

You Will Need

Measuring tape	Iron
Fabric	Trim
Lining	Buckram
Scissors	Straight pins
Sewing machine and thread	Drapery hooks

1
Lay out the fabric and cut to size according to the dimensions desired for your drapes (see sidebar). Cut the lining fabric to the same width measurements as the panel, but 1 inch shorter in length so the lining doesn't show below the drape when hung (photo A).

2
Turn up and sew a double 4-inch hem on both the panel and the lining (photo B). (See page 14.)

3
Cut the valance fabric and the lining to the same width as the drapery fabric and to the desired height, adding about ½ inch for the seam allowance.

4
Place the valance fabric and lining right sides together. Pin in place, and sew across the bottom using a ⅝-inch seam allowance.

SIZING DRAPES

Getting the right dimensions for your drapes requires careful measuring and a little math. Standard pleated drapes have five to seven pleats, and they begin 2½ inches from each side of the panel.

1
Measure the window to determine the finished size of the drapery panels.

2
Add 9 inches to the length—8 inches for the hem and 1 inch for the seam allowance.

3
To determine the width, decide how many pleats you will have. Using 5 pleats, there will be four spaces between the pleats and 2½ inches on each side of the pleats.

4
To allow extra fabric for the gather of each pleat, multiply the width of the curtain rod by 1½, or for an extra-full look, multiply the width by 3. Then add about 1 inch to the width for the seam allowances as well.

5 Turn the fabric right side out (photo C) and press. Turn under 1 inch along the sides and top and press. Attach the trim along the bottom of the right side of the valance.

6 Place the panel fabric right side up on the work table. Lay the valance right side up across the panel. Place the panel lining with the right side facing down on top of the valance (photo D).

7 Cut the buckram to the width of the drapery panel, and slip it under all three layers (photo E). Pin all of the layers to the buckram. This will provide stiffening at the top of the drape.

8 Sew all four layers together across the top with a $5/8$-inch seam allowance. Flip the lining over and press across the top.

9 Fold a double 1½-inch seam down each side (photo F); press and sew the hem.

10 Measure the total width of the panel, subtract 5 inches (for the 2½ inches on each side of the pleats) and divide the remaining total by 4 (four spaces between each pleat). This is how far apart to make the pleats.

11 Measure 2½ inches from the edge and mark with a pin (photo G). Then measure the appropriate distance for the pleat (according to the measurement in step 12) and place a second pin. Mark all of the pleats and spaces, at equal distances, with pins across the top of the panel.

12 Fold the material over, matching pin to pin, for the first pleat (photo H). Sew down the pleat at the pin from the top to the bottom of the buckram, about 4 to 5 inches (photo I). Repeat for each pleat.

13 Pinch the fold of the pleat and push toward the seam, dividing the pleat into thirds (photo J), pinching the layers together and pinning at the bottom to hold the pleat in place.

14 Sew from the folded edge of the pleat across the width of the pleat to its seam (photo K).

15 Slide drapery hooks onto the back of each pleat (photo L) and attach to the drapery rod.

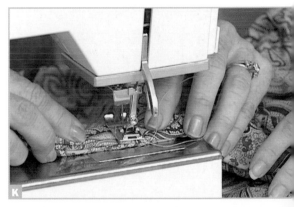

TIPS | DIY Network Crafts

ALLOWING FOR SEAMS

A standard seam allowance in sewing is $5/8$ inch. When instructions call for adding "about $1/2$ inch" to allow for seams, it is for simplicity. To be precise, add $5/8$ inch for one seam or $1\frac{1}{4}$ inches for two seams to a fabric dimension.

LEATHER DESK TOPPER

Create a new desktop to cover a desk you already have and give it a whole new look. In this project, the desk topper extends the work surface as well. Make the top from a sheet of plywood, cover it with faux leather, and stud the edges with brass nail stud strips for a handsome desk renovation.

You Will Need

Measuring tape	Staple gun and staples
¾" plywood	Brass nail stud trim
Faux leather fabric	Wire cutter
Scissors	Hammer

1 Measure the fabric to the size of the plywood piece, adding a few extra inches to each side and cut.

2 Lay the fabric out on the work surface, right side down, smoothing it out completely. Center the plywood onto the wrong side of the fabric (photo A).

3 Use a staple gun to attach the fabric to the plywood. Staple the long sides first, starting in the center (photo B). Pull the fabric to fit smoothly around the edge of the plywood, but avoiding stretching it out of shape. Continue stapling each side, stopping a few inches from the corners.

TIPS | DIY Network Crafts

PRE-CUT PLYWOOD

Measure the desk top and have your plywood cut to size when you buy it, adding additional length or width if you want to extend your work surface.

4 To finish the corner, trim away the excess fabric, fold, and staple in place (photo C).

5 Add brass nail studs and trim around the edges. This comes in strips with a hole every few inches to secure to upholstery. Cut the strip with a wire cutter so it begins with a hole to secure the strip to the corner of the desk topper.

6 Position the nail strip on the edge of the covered plywood and use a hammer to tap a nail stud into the hole provided (photo D). Continue around the edge of the plywood, keeping the strip level. At the corner, gently bend the strip and continue nailing. If your desk topper will be against a wall, apply nail strips only to the front and sides.

TIPS | DIY Network Crafts

◢ PERFECT TRIM

If the nail strip does not end with a hole at the corner, cut a short section of the strip with a hole at the end. Overlap the cut section with the strip already in place, positioning the hole at the corner. Nail in place.

◢ TIGHT FINISH

If the fabric is not taut across the wood after stapling, push the excess up to the line of staples, creating a small fold. Staple on the other side of the fold to take up the slack (photo below).

FINISHING TOUCHES

To finish off the look of your home office, light up an old lamp by wrapping the lampshade in an animal print or other fabric (see Covered Lamp Shade, page 26), add pillows for color and texture (see Pieced Designer Pillows, page 37, and Tufted Round Pillow, page 36), and make a custom table runner (see Table Runner, page 28).

COZY STUDY

With their only child leaving for college, Alan and Rebecca were about to be alone in a big home. They wanted a comfortable space to retreat to that wouldn't feel like they were rattling around in an empty house.

BEFORE: Ordinary and crowded with family effects, this study did not have the peaceful, welcoming feel the homeowners wanted.

PROJECT SUMMARY

The Material Girls used a warm palette of reds, greens, and golds to create a cozy study for these homeowners to enjoy. They updated an old bookcase with fabric panels, gave an old chair a new look with a faux slipcover, and created reversible curtains to change with the seasons.

Fabric and Color Swatches

AFTER: (Right) Fabric backing for a bookcase and a table runner for the desk add texture and warmth to previously cold surfaces.

(Left) A faux slipcover for a comfortable chair and reversible curtains create a place to curl up and read.

◤ ARMCHAIR FAUX SLIPCOVER ◢

Using a table runner and a staple gun, this chair cover is an easy and quick transformation with a French country layered look.

You Will Need

Arm chair	Staple gun and staples
Measuring tape	Hook-and-loop tape
Fabric runner	

1 To take the dimensions of the chair, remove the seat cushion. Starting just under the front of the chair (photo A), measure every angle—over the top, down the back, and just under the bottom. Add a few inches to the length to be able to secure the fabric underneath.

2 Using the measurements from step 1, cut out the fabric and stitch the runner (see page 28).

3 Tilt the chair forward to work on the back first. Fold the end of the runner under the back bottom edge and staple to the bottom of the chair, starting at the center and working out (photo B).

4 Wrap the fabric up and over the top and down the front of the chair, smoothing it out as you go. Tuck any excess fabric into the folds of the chair, both on the sides and at the seat (photo C).

5 Wrap the runner under the bottom of the chair, fold for a hem, and secure with staples (photo D).

6 Measure around the seat cushion (photo E), adding several inches for hemming. Cut and sew another runner to cover the cushion from front to back around the top and bottom.

7 Sew hook-and-loop tape to each end of the cushion cover fabric. Wrap the cover around the seat cushion and secure (photo F).

TIPS | DIY Network Crafts

WORKING WITH WINGBACKS

Since a wingback chair is higher at the middle back, be sure to measure the center top of the chair. Wingbacks are also wider at the top and narrower at the seat, so taper the material in a few inches on each side. After the chair is wrapped, fold in the excess fabric on the top sides of the wingback and hand stitch it in place.

REVERSIBLE CURTAINS

Make these curtains with tab tops so that when it's time to reverse them, you can just flip the rod over from side to side.

You Will Need

2 decorative fabrics	Straight pins
Scissors	Trim or gimp
Measuring tape	Iron
Sewing machine and thread	Curtain rod

1 Cut one piece of fabric from each fabric according to your measurements (photo A). If you are sewing multiple curtain panels with a patterned print, be sure to match the fabrics when cutting (see page 44).

2 Place both fabrics right sides together and pin around the edges. Sew around all sides, leaving the top side open. Snip all corners (photo B) so the fabric will pop out and lay flat after turning.

3 Turn the curtain right side out, turning out the corners as well, and press for nice, crisp seams.

4 Tuck in the raw edges at the top of the curtain by 1 inch (photo C). Press the top hem in place.

5 Determine how far apart you want the curtain tabs and how many you will need. Cut the trim to the desired length for the tabs.

A

B

6 Fold the trim strips in half and pin them at equal distances along the top of the curtain (photo D). Sew the top opening closed (photo E).

7 Run the curtain rod through the tabs to hang the curtain. To reverse the curtain, simply lift the rod from the bracket and flip to the other side.

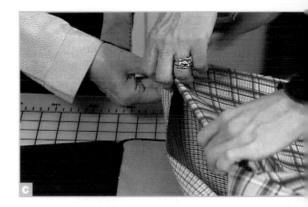

TIPS | DIY Network Crafts

TIE-BACKS

For added style, purchase tie-backs in coordinating colors to tie the curtains open.

MEASURING FOR CURTAINS

For floor-length curtains, measure from the top of the curtain rod to the floor. Then add 1 to 2 inches, depending on the size of the rod. Measure the width of the curtain rod to determine how many panels you will need for the desired fullness. For a tailored, flat-panel look, use your measurements as taken. For a standard fullness, multiply the width by 1½; for an extra-full look, multiply by 3. Finally add 1 inch to both the length and width for the seam allowance.

BOOKCASE BACK PANEL

Using foam core and fabric, create a fabric panel to place behind the shelves and give an old bookcase a fresh new look.

You Will Need

- Bookcase with removable shelves
- Measuring tape
- Foam core
- Fabric
- Scissors
- Staple gun and staples

1 Remove the shelves from the bookcase and measure the height and width of the inside of the bookcase (photo A), and cut the foam to size.

2 Using the foam core as a pattern, cut the fabric to size, adding 2 inches all the way around (photo B).

3 Wrap the fabric around the foam core and staple it on the backside, using short staples so you don't go through the foam core. Start at the center of each side (photo C), and work your way to the corners. Save the corners for last.

4 At the corners, fold the extra fabric and staple it down (photo D).

5 Insert the back panel into the bookcase, supporting it on the base shelf (photo E). Put the remaining shelves into place.

▨ BOOKCASE CURTAINS ▨

Curtains on the lower shelves of a bookcase provide a place to hide clutter. Make two curtain panels for easier access to the shelves.

You Will Need

Bookcase	Ruler
Measuring tape	Fusible tape
Fabric	Iron
Scissors	Hook-and-loop tape

1 Measure the height and width of the area on the bookcase to be covered by the curtain. Divide the width by 2, for two curtains. Add 1 inch on each side for the seam allowance.

2 Cut the fabric according to the measurements, matching the fabric if necessary (see page 44). Use a ruler to help cut the edges as straight as possible so the curtains will hang evenly. Turn the edges under and press (photo A).

3 Lay a piece of fusible tape under the edge of the fabric (photo B). Press the edge of the fabric with a hot iron for 5 to 10 seconds to cause the tape to fuse, creating a hem. Miter the corners and use fusible tape to secure them as well.

4 Attach hook-and-loop tape to the backside of the top of the curtain panel and the other to the bookcase shelf. This makes the curtain easy to remove or to switch with others for a new look.

FINISHING TOUCHES

Add a table runner to soften a desk (see Table Runner, page 28) and a matching chair cushion. Cover lampshades (see Covered Lamp Shade, page 26) in coordinating fabric.

TIPS | DIY Network Crafts

EVEN HEMS

To help keep the side hems straight, measure across the panel and use painter's tape to mark the fold edge all of the way across. Turn it under, press lightly, and then remove the painter's tape.

WARM COUNTRY KITCHEN

Joe and Sarah moved into a new home and the kitchen and its dining area needed a little help. They wanted to add some color and comfort to the room to transform it from its "contractor taupe" into something more warm and welcoming.

BEFORE: This new kitchen was bland and lacking personality.

AFTER: A new tablecloth, room screen, and handmade candle tray for a centerpiece give the room warmth and charm.

Fabric and Color Swatches

◣ PROJECT SUMMARY ◢

The Material Girls used an array of earth-tone fabrics in a warm traditional style to transform this kitchen's dining space into the heart of the home. They sewed a round, scalloped tablecloth for the kitchen table, made a candle-holder centerpiece, and constructed a room screen.

AFTER: Both the hutch (right) and the corner screen (above) help soften the corners of the kitchen's dining area.

◤ ROUND TABLE TOPPER ◢

Make a custom, scalloped tablecloth with cording added along the edge for a graceful table cover.

You Will Need

Round table	Fabric chalk	Sewing machine and thread
Measuring tape	Lining	Painter's paper
Calculator (optional)	Scissors	Cording
Fabric	Serger or pinking shears	Iron
Ruler	Straight pins	

1 Measure the diameter of your table. Add an extra inch for the seam allowance. Then multiply by pi (3.14) to calculate the circumference. In this project, the table diameter was 55 inches. The calculation was 55 inches plus 1 inch for the seam allowance, times 3.14 for a circumference of 176 inches.

2 Quarter the fabric by folding it in half and then folding it in half again. With the fold facing toward you, place a measuring tape at the corner of the fold and measure down half the distance of the table measurement. (In this case, half of 56 is 28 inches.)

3 Use the ruler as a guide and mark from one end of the folded material to the other end with fabric chalk (photo A). Cut along the chalk line through all layers.

4 Repeat steps 2 and 3 with the lining fabric and cut. Serge the fabric and lining together, or use pinking shears to cut the edges.

5 To make the scalloped piece, first create a pattern out of painter's paper. Use a plate in the size for the scallops (see sidebar Calculating Scallops) and trace around it, drawing out the scallop pattern on the painter's paper. Cut out the pattern.

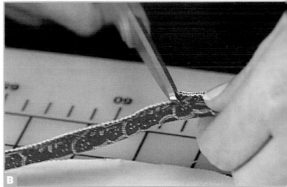

6 Lay the pattern onto the tablecloth fabric and trace around the scallops with fabric chalk. Cut along the chalk line. Repeat with the lining material.

7 Lay the scalloped fabric and its lining with right sides together. Clip the seam allowance of the cording every few inches to help it lay flat (photo B). Tuck the cording between the fabric layers and pin.

8 Sew a straight stitch around the edge of the cording at the top of the scallop (photo C). Clip the cording again in the corners of the scallops, if necessary, for the cording to lay flat.

9 Pin the scalloped piece to the edge of the table top with right sides together (photo D). Sew a straight stitch all the way around. Press the hem for a crisp look.

CALCULATING SCALLOPS

In order to have scallops meet perfectly, choose a number by which the circumference of the table is divisible. Just divide the circumference by various numbers until you find one that goes in evenly and will be an appropriate size for a scallop. In this case the circumference was 176 inches, and the size of the scallop was 11 inches.

CANDLE CENTERPIECE

Use wood, fabric, and decorative nail head trim to make this kitchen candle centerpiece.

You Will Need

Wood (precut to desired size)	Scissors
Measuring tape	Staple gun and staples
Drill	Brass nail stud trim
Cabinet door pulls	Hammer
Fabric	Pillar candles

1 Measure and mark in ¾ inch from all four corners on the pre-cut wood.

2 Drill a hole at each mark and screw the cabinet door pulls in place to create the feet for the centerpiece (photo A).

3 Lay the fabric right side down and lay the wood on top of it. Cut the fabric around the wood, allowing several extra inches on each side to allow for stapling.

4 Starting in the center of one edge of the wood, tightly pull the fabric around it and staple in place.

5 At the knobs, cut a slit in the fabric (photo B), fold the edges in, and staple around the knob. Neatly fold the corners (like wrapping a package) before stapling (photo C).

6 Use brass nail stud trim around the sides of the centerpiece. Lay the trim along the edge and secure it with nails through the holes using a hammer (photo D). Set the candles in place on the centerpiece.

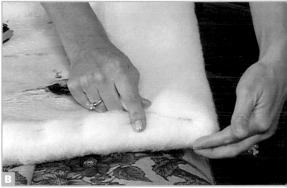

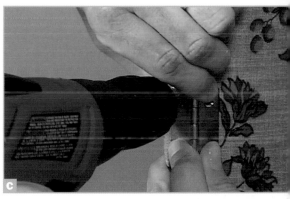

ROOM SCREEN

Cover two wood panels with fabric, hinge them together, and add the same decorative brass nail head trim used on the centerpiece for a coordinating accent for the kitchen. Batting underneath the fabric gives a more dramatic, fuller look to the screen.

You Will Need

Batting	Brass nail head trim
3 6" x 14" wood frames	Hammer
Staple gun and staples	3 hinges
Scissors	Screwdriver
Fabric	

1 Wrap the batting tightly around one wood frame. Starting in the center, staple the batting all the way around the frame (photo A).

2 Neatly fold the corners and staple into place (photo B). Cut off any excess batting. Repeat with the other two wood frames.

3 Repeat the same process with the fabric, matching up the prints on each frame. (See Matching the Fabric Pattern, page 44.)

4 Add brass nail head trim around the edges of the frame, taking care to keep the strip of trim very straight as you go. Install nails into the holes on the trim with a hammer.

5 Set hinges 12 inches from the top and bottom of the screen and in the center. Attach the hinges to the frames with screws (photo C).

◢ DINNER NAPKINS ◣

Choose contrasting fabrics for these napkins to give your table a change of color.

You Will Need

2 decorative fabrics	Straight pins
Measuring tape	Sewing machine and thread
Fabric chalk	Iron
Scissors	

1 Mark and cut both fabrics into 16-inch squares (photo A). Lay contrasting fabrics with right sides together.

2 Pin in place, and sew a ½-inch seam on all sides (photo B). Leave an opening to turn the napkin right side out. Clip the corners.

3 Turn the napkin right side out and press, folding under the edges of the opening. Topstitch with a straight stitch all the way around the napkin (photo C).

TIPS | DIY Network Crafts

FILLING TRIM GAPS

If your strip of trim is not long enough to complete the job, fill in with a short length of additional trim. Cut a piece of trim with a nail hole in a center position. Place the patch to overlap the trim on each side and nail into place.

FINISHING TOUCHES

Add a runner in coordinating fabric on top of the new tablecloth and to the bar (see Table Runner, page 28). Hang café curtains at each window and fabric wall art (see Painted Fabric Wall Art, page 87) to add warmth to a blank space.

ACKNOWLEDGMENTS

Special thanks to everyone at Rivr Media, the production company for the *Material Girls* TV show, including Dee Haslam, Shelly White, Dara Canada, and Lauren Justice. Thanks also to Trudy Dinnhaupt and Mary Pintaro for their contributions to the interior designs found in this book.